KidShapes

KidShapes

A GUIDE TO HELPING YOUR KIDS
CONTROL THEIR WEIGHT

Laura Walther Nathanson, M.D., FAAP

HarperCollins*Publishers*

This book contains advice and information relating to health and dietary care for children. It is not intended to replace medical advice and should be used to supplement rather than replace regular care by your child's pediatrician. Since every child is different, you should consult your child's pediatrician on questions specific to your child.

HarperCollins books may be purchased for educational, business, or sales promotional use. For information, please write to: Special Markets Department, HarperCollins Publishers, Inc., 10 East 53rd Street, New York, NY 10022.

FIRST EDITION

Designed by Helene Wald Berinsky

Library of Congress Cataloging-in-Publication Data

Nathanson, Laura.
    Kidshapes : a guide to helping your kids control their weight / Laura Walther Nathanson. — 1st ed.
      p. cm.
    Includes bibliographical references and index.
    ISBN 0-06-270135-5
    1. Children—Nutrition. 2. Obesity in children—Prevention. 3. Infants—Nutrition. 4. Children—Nutrition—Psychological aspects. I. Title.
RJ206.N258   1995
613.2'083—dc20   95-1797

95 96 97 98 99 ❖/RRD 10 9 8 7 6 5 4 3 2 1

To Sara's grandparents:
the memory of the ones who missed knowing her,
Sara and Roy Walther, and the kindness of the ones
whom we are delighted to have with us,
Marian and Ben Nathanson.

Contents

Acknowledgments

I can't thank enough:

Chuck, for too many things to mention; Sara, for being Sara; my partners and the entire staff at El Camino Pediatrics for patience, kindness, professionalism, and fun; and my pediatric colleagues, especially at Children's Hospital, UCSD Medical Center, Sharp Hospital, and Scripps Hospitals in La Jolla and Encinitas, for all kinds of support; also, librarians Janis Emmert and Esther Pusich!

Louie Linarelli, M.D., pediatric endocrinologist, for reading and commenting on the manuscript and for taking good care of the children I send to him.

Kathy James, DNSc, for reading Chapter 5 and for taking good care of the children I send to her Shapedown program, which she does so well.

The children on the cover (and their parents): Allison Bauer, David Beauchaine, Alex Martinez, and Megan Meyer; and Marshall Harrington for taking such a snappy shot.

Rob Kaplan, for being a terrific editor; Judy Tashbook and Aileen Boyles, for being sunny, energetic publicists; and Sandra Dijkstra and crew, for doing what agents are supposed to do with such flair and pizzazz.

Joe Sweeney, for his fitness counseling for Chuck and me.

In my opinion, they are all in the 100th percentile.

Preface

THE STATISTICS OF BABY FAT

- One in four American children is overweight. In the age group of six to eleven years, that's 4 million children.
- An obese infant has a 10 percent chance of becoming an obese adult. For obese preschoolers the chance is 25 percent, for obese seven-year-olds it is 40 percent, and for obese eleven-year-olds it is 75 percent.
- If one parent is obese, a child has a 40 percent chance of becoming obese. If both parents are obese, a child has an 80 percent chance of becoming obese.
- Americans have reduced their physical activity by 75 percent and increased fats in the diet by 31 percent since 1900.
- Most overly chubby children gain the extra fat gradually. Fifty extra calories a day that aren't burned off in growth and exercise can add up to five extra pounds in a year. One hundred extra calories adds up to ten pounds. That's a lot for a young child.
- Dieting to lose weight in childhood almost never works—80 to 90 percent of children who lose weight regain to their previous degree of chubbiness. Growing into the extra weight is much more effective.

When I examine young bellies, I pretend to detect what was eaten for the previous meal or two or three. Today I am making a big production of it with a particularly ticklish Seven: snapping on the gloves, rubbing the hands together, then frowning into the distance as I poke and pry.

"Here's a, uh, a powdered doughnut," I said, "and a piece of pizza with pineapple, anchovies, and onions; way down here are two Oreo cookies with the frosting licked off separately; here's three dill pickles; here's a chocolate milk, and oh—right down here is a peanut butter sandwich with grape jelly!"

I come out of my fake trance to find Cassidy and her mother staring at me.

"You got everything right!" her mother exclaims, clearly awestruck. "Except for the pizza."

"Yeah," says Cassidy. "I don't like the little fishies. Those were green peppers."

Well. I'm good, but I'm not that good. My "discoveries" are based on studies that show what children in America eat. I'm not surprised at all to have guessed everything right. (You always take a chance with the dill pickles, but Cassidy smells a little garlicky.) I'm not surprised, either, to find pickles, pineapple chunks, and apple juice—and green pepper slices—the only vegetables represented.

No, I'm not surprised. But I am concerned. Cassidy, at Seven, is starting to gain more weight than is good for her. She's not alone.

And the question is, what to do?

Some pediatricians would hesitate even to give such vague and generalized guidelines as "try to increase exercise" and "try to watch the sweets and fats." Many would reassure parents that children will "grow out of it." Hardly any would give a number to the extra pounds or make specific suggestions on lifestyle changes.

That's because there's a big and well-recognized fear: We don't want to give Cassidy any signals that she is too fat, that we don't love her, that she is not a wonderful kid. We don't want Cassidy preoccupied with calories, feeling deprived, feeling different.

We pediatricians also don't want to give *parents* any negative signals about Cassidy or her weight.

A campaign against extra weight all too often turns into a campaign to lose weight, with the emphasis on restricting food portions as well as food types. This would be a mistake. For one thing, a restricted diet could deny her essential nutrition. Cassie could become iron- or calcium- or vitamin-deficient. For another, we know from a multitude of studies that *reducing* diets don't work and, indeed, backfire: 80 to 90 percent of children put on such diets return to their previous degree of overweight.

Worse, such a campaign can make food and weight the focus of a family's life and of a child's sense of worth. We strongly suspect that this kind of campaign may be one of the triggers of malignant eating disorders, like anorexia nervosa.

It's no wonder that as pediatricians we have more or less opted out of guiding parents and children on the issue of overweight.

But I fear that in opting out, we haven't helped, and we may have caused more trouble. We don't calm anxiety by ignoring the issue: We increase it.

We certainly aren't helping America's children to attain and maintain appropriate weight ranges. One study showed that from 1963 to 1980, obesity rose 54 percent in six- to eleven-year-olds. In fact, statistics suggest that as many as one in four school-age children is truly overweight, and one in five teenagers, and one in three adults. Although many overweight children do not go on to become obese teenagers or adults, some do. Statistics don't tell us anything about an individual child.

Being considerably different in size and shape is hard on youngsters emotionally. Their day-to-day lives become more difficult, and they may become preoccupied with this issue, distracted from more fruitful challenges and deprived of many pleasures.

When parents and children do not get honest assessments about overweight, they are left to their own intuitions about whether or not chubbiness is a problem. Very often these assessments are off base in either direction. Some studies show that 80 percent of prepubertal and just-pubertal girls believe—falsely— that they weigh too much. At the other extreme, every pediatrician has talked with parents who feel that their slightly chubby child is too thin, and that they have failed as parents in "getting him to eat."

If we don't tell parents what is appropriate, how are they supposed to know?

This very uncertainty produces anxiety and a lack of self-confidence. Nothing could be more undermining to the efforts of caring, intelligent parents.

Fomenting this anxiety is a culture that flagrantly offers an incredible array of rich, affordable, habit-forming foods at the same time that it idealizes thinness. Children and adults who inherit a metabolism that burns off surplus calories are at a distinct advantage in such a society. Because we intuitively associate "burning off calories" with goal-directed activity, we actually attribute virtue to thinness. Nobody points out that most of that "burning off" doesn't go into exercise or even activity. It's "waste disposal" burning.

Alas, even when it is obvious that a child is becoming increasingly chubby, specific, clear, calm advice is often not forthcoming. Nutrition consults usually aren't covered by insurance policies unless the child is dangerously overweight. Even many nutritionists who are consulted privately are reluctant to suggest cutting calories.

Parents, ever more anxious, try one thing after another. They may try to accept the pediatrician's reassurances, and then become guilt-ridden and angry as the child's weight continues to accrue. They may institute their own restrictions on food choices and quantities and then become frightened that these measures may backfire or precipitate an eating disorder. They fuss and scold and nag, and then they repent and expend enormous energies restraining the impulse to fuss, scold, and nag.

All too often, this preoccupation takes over the whole family, and they come to regard the child's extra weight as The Enemy. When children sense this, there's trouble.

In the logic of childhood, kids may feel that casting a larger shadow means that they are taking up too much room in the world. It's hard for a child to understand that the "room" one "takes up" has a lot more to do with qualities like kindness and honesty and humor and sensitivity and courage than with how much one weighs.

All this anxiety and distress can distort parent–child relationships and get in the way of the healthy development of trust, independence, and esteem. It certainly gets in the way of fun.

What parents in this situation need is advice that does not falsely reassure, that is clear and rational and safe and effective, and that is delivered in a manner that does not feed into anxiety but rather calms it.

Here is what I think parents want and need, and what I have tried to provide:

• How to tell whether your child of a given age is over the "just right" range of weight for height, taking into account body build and muscular development.
• How to help a child who is over his or her own range to grow into the extra weight over time, and how to tell how long it will take.
• How to help children, in general, form habits of exercise and eating that will help them stay "just right" during adolescence and adulthood.
• How to take advantage of each developmental stage in this endeavor.

When the whole subject loses its mystery, I hope and believe that parents and children will feel less anxious and less inclined to treat extra weight as The Enemy. That should free up a lot of time and energy for other, more pleasant pursuits.

As for Cassidy, see what happens in Chapter 5, "School-age Kids: Five to Puberty."

THE FACTS OF "BABY FAT"

What parents should know about growth in childhood:

- Only rarely does excess weight mean a hormonal or other problem. When there is an underlying medical cause, children are not only overly chubby but are almost always short and show other physical and developmental signs of an underlying disorder.
- Between the ages of two and about ten, children normally don't gain much weight each year. For instance, through age six, most children gain only about four and one-half pounds a year—that's just six ounces a month.
- During this age span, children normally are picky eaters. A good breakfast, a fair lunch, and not much dinner is a normal pattern.
- Normally, from age two to age ten, children do not make new fat cells. If children gain too rapidly during these years, they don't just expand the fat cells, they make new ones: cells that are there for life.
- For girls, adolescence is a period of rapid weight gain. Chubby girls should not be told that puberty will help them slim down; the reverse is true. Girls who gain extra weight as fat tend to mature—reach puberty—earlier.
- The ages at which very young children are most likely to gain too much fat are between one and two for girls and between two and three and between four and six for boys. For school-age children, the most likely age is between six and nine years.
- Chubby children should grow into extra weight by slowing or nearly stopping weight gain as they grow in height. A seven-year-old will need at least a year to a year and a half to grow into each extra 20 percent of weight.

KidShapes

Getting Started: An Introduction

How and why do some children gain too much weight?

There are zillions of studies on all aspects of this question. In other words, nobody really knows. But we're clear on this: Genes determine how likely a child is to become overweight in an environment that allows that to happen. And if ever there were such an environment at any time in the world's history, it's ours in America, right now.

Most children who gain more weight than nature intended are not lazy, nor do they binge. Nor do they grow up in miserable, dysfunctional families. On the contrary: They lead perfectly normal, indeed often exemplary, lives. But they take in a small number of calories more than they burn off in growth and activity, and they do this on a regular basis over weeks, months, years.

Of course, that's not the whole story. What kind of calories are taken in makes a difference—fat calories versus protein versus carbohydrate. How you burn them up makes a difference—aerobic versus non-aerobic activity, swimming versus exercise that defies gravity, and so on.

We don't know exactly how genes play a role. Maybe they govern appetite and the sense of fullness, or influence whether somebody likes to exercise or would prefer not to, or help to set the thermostat on the internal furnace that controls how we burn calories. Some children may have an inherited tendency to use surplus food very efficiently, turning any extra calories into fat rather than burning them off as extra energy. No doubt this was a big genetic advantage in human history. It probably saw a large number of ancestors through famines and tough winters and multiple pregnancies. In today's America, though, it's a big disadvantage.

It's hard to believe that genes alone account for the numbers of American children who are overweight. When people whose culture reinforces slenderness immigrate here, they too become vulnerable to overweight; yet they have the same old genes. As a population, we are getting more and more overweight—and we have the same old genes, too; the genetic composition does not change in fifty or one hundred years. It seems far more likely that the situation has to do with the fact that our society as a whole has reduced physical activity by 75 percent since 1900 and in the same time period increased the amount of fat in our diet by 31 percent.

After all, genes don't determine how much and what kind of food is available, or whether there is exercise so bound up in daily life that it's unavoidable—or so attractive that it's irresistible.

Fortunately, we as parents and pediatricians don't need to enter into the arcane realms of biochemistry and genetics. What we need to do is design an environment which makes it likely that a child will gain the weight that nature intends for today's world, not the world of the frozen tundra or the sere savannah.

How can you tell whether your child is in his or her "just right" range?

- You can eyeball the child. And you can watch how he or she moves. You can see if the child feels self-conscious or find out if he or she is being teased about weight.
- You can measure height and weight and "put the child on the growth chart."
- You can obtain a measurement of how much extra fat there is by using special calipers to measure a fold of fat,

usually under a shoulder blade, and putting that measurement on a chart specific for the age and sex of the child.

Each of these is tricky. Used alone, each can lead to disaster. But if you combine "eyeballing" with one of the other methods, you usually can get an idea. And then have your idea confirmed by your pediatrician.

EYEBALLING

At each age up to puberty, there is a typical shape. That's the shape of the average-build girl or boy who is of average weight for height. It reflects the amount of padding such a child has. When you "eyeball" a child for overweight, it is this typical child you use for comparison.

There are lots of traps here.

First, you have to have an idea of what the typical child looks like at each age. That means you have to have seen a lot of normal-weight children and identified that shape in your mind as "typical."

Parents may not often see large groups of children the same age as their own. Many children are dropped off at day-care centers or schools by parents who get only a quick glimpse of the other children. Moreover, when 25 percent of American children are overweight, our eyes adjust to those we see. When they do, a plump child looks typical, and a truly "typical" one looks skinny. Then a slender one looks emaciated, and one who weighs quite a lot more than nature intends can look just a bit on the chubby side.

Second, you need to be aware of the normal range of variation. There will be some variation among races and between sexes. One child may carry an extra 10 percent of body weight as bone or muscle; another may carry that much as fat.

Third, some children are designed by nature to be more padded and rounded than others. How can you tell this normal extra padding from "more weight than nature intended"? You need a practiced and dispassionate eye. You also need one of the formal measurements discussed in the following paragraphs.

GROWTH CHARTS

Most people are absolutely spooked by charts. No wonder. There's something about "putting a child on the growth chart" that reminds one of pinning the tail on the donkey: It's done in the dark, and where you wind up depends largely on luck.

This attitude is not an option for parents who want to help their child who is at high risk for extra chubbiness.

Fortunately, this feeling about charts is a bum rap. They are not that hard to deal with if you take them step by step and don't panic.

FEELING AT HOME WITH GROWTH CHARTS

Growth charts are not warm and fuzzy, but they are not hard to use once you get the hang of them. I suggest that you read this section rather than study it, just sort of getting the gist of how growth charts work. Then as we come to individual children in each chapter, you'll become more and more at home with the charts.

Basically, the charts tell us how a particular child compares in height or weight with a normal population of other children. For instance, one chart tells us how tall a boy or girl is compared with children of the same age. Another tells us how much a boy or girl weighs compared with others the same age. A third tells us how much a boy or girl weighs compared with others of the same height.

To find the chart you want to use, look at the two scales of numbers, one going along the bottom and the other going up along the side. Make sure the chart is labeled for your child's sex and age, too.

If the scale along the bottom is age, the chart is looking at height or weight according to age. If the scale along the bottom is height, then the chart is looking at weight according to height.

All the charts depend on a concept called "percentiles."

When you look at a chart, you see that it consists of lines going up from left to right. These lines are labeled 5, 10, 25, 50, 75, 90, and 95.

With each chart, you find your child's "numbers" along the bottom scale and along the side scale. For instance, find your child's age along the bottom and his or her height or weight along the side. Draw a line straight up from your child's age at the bottom, and a line straight sideways from the height or weight at the side. Find where those lines intersect, and make a dot at that point.

That dot will be either on a percentile line, between two percentile lines, below the 5th percentile, or above the 95th percentile. If that dot or point is at the 50th percentile, that means your child is right in the middle of whatever is being measured. For instance, if your child is in the 50th percentile for height, it means that if you lined your child up with 100 randomly chosen children of the same sex and age, 50 of those children would be taller and 50 would be shorter than your child.

If your child's dot or point is at the 90th percentile for height, it means that if you lined your child up with 100 randomly chosen children of the same sex and age, 90 would be shorter and only 10 would be taller than your child.

Here's what confuses most people about the charts.

• The Height for Age and Weight for Age charts are on the same sheet. The height percentile lines are on the top and the weight percentile lines are on the bottom. Be careful you don't mix up the scales along the side!
• Here is what will make this easier. *Just don't pay any attention to the bottom scale on that page—the Weight for Age scale.* It doesn't give us any useful information. Who cares what your child weighs compared to other children his or her age? Some of the children your child's age are very tall and should weigh more. Some are very short and should weigh less. Why should we want to compare them by age?
• Instead, find the chart with the height scale along the bottom

and weight scale along the side. That's the scale that will tell us whether a child weighs an unusual amount for his or her height.

- Again, make sure you've got the appropriate chart for your child's sex and age. They are all labeled, of course, but it's surprisingly easy to get confused.
- Don't confuse inches and centimeters when you are looking at the height scale or pounds and kilograms when you are looking at the weight scale.

As you can see, we aren't comparing a particular child to some mythical Perfectly Normal Child. What we are doing when we use the growth charts is comparing a particular child to a large population of children. The number of children studied was so large, and their racial and economic backgrounds so varied, that the charts give us a pretty good idea of a "normal range" of height for age and of weight for height. If a child grows within that normal range, usually all is well.

What is the normal range of height for age?

The normal range for height for a given child is that determined by his or her genes and reflecting normal medical health. A normal child can grow along any of the percentile lines for height.

Of course, there are some perfectly healthy children who are "off the chart" for height—taller than the 95th percentile or shorter than the 5th percentile. Indeed, that's what the chart says: that 5 percent of normal children are taller and 5 percent of normal children are shorter than those percentiles.

After the first year or so of life, however, we expect a child to stick pretty closely to a given percentile line as he or she grows in height. Suddenly not growing, or suddenly shooting up in height long before puberty is expected, can be a warning sign of a medical problem.

What is a normal range for weight?

Remember, we are not using the chart that looks at weight

for age. We are using the chart that looks at weight for height or length.

To use this chart, find your child's height on the scale along the bottom and weight on the scale along the side. Draw the straight lines out from these points and see where they intersect.

If that point is between the 25th and 75th percentile, you can be pretty sure that your child is neither too thin nor too fat, but Just Right.

If your child's point falls between the 5th and the 25th percentile, your child is probably still perfectly healthy—just very slender or lightly built.

But if your child's point is below the 5th percentile, your child is much thinner than average. More than 95 percent of all children his or her height weigh more than your child does. Often, this is perfectly normal, but your pediatrician should check it out.

If your child's point falls between the 75th and 90th percentile, your child could be too chubby—or he or she could be very muscular or have a very large build with heavy bones.

If your child's point falls at or above the 90th percentile, the chance of your child's being too chubby is very great. The farther over the 95th percentile that point is, the more overly chubby the child. It is very rare for a child to weigh that much more than the average child and have that extra weight be due to muscles or bones.

Most importantly, it is trends over time rather than a single point that parents and pediatricians should watch. If a child has always been at the 75th percentile but then jumps to the 90th, then something has changed to add extra weight. Is it muscle, from a new athletic involvement? Or fat, because of a change in lifestyle?

The Weight for Height chart helps to flag trends. Then parents and pediatricians work together as detectives to see what's going on.

Alas, many pediatricians do not use the Weight for Height chart, but the Weight for Age chart. It is very inviting to do so, since it's on the same page as the Height for Age chart. But it's not a good idea. The Weight for Age chart can be very deceiving, and can disguise the fact that a child is becoming much too chubby until the situation has become difficult to correct. The earlier we spot a Chubbiness Trend, the better. After all, we don't want children to have to lose extra weight but rather to grow into the extra weight, just slowing down the rate of gain. The more time they have to do this before puberty, the easier it is.

If you visit your pediatrician with concerns about chubbiness, be sure to clarify which chart you are using. It can make a big difference, particularly after age Six. To see how, let's look at Jenny and Nancy.

Jenny's Growth Charts

Here are the charts of my friends Jenny and Nancy. They show why it is better to use the Weight for Height chart instead of the Weight for Age chart.

HEIGHT FOR AGE

We find Jenny's age in years along the scale at the bottom of the chart, and her height at each age in the Inches scale along the left-hand side. We draw lines from each set of measurements and find where they intersect. Each time, they intersect at the 90th percentile. This means that all through these years, Jenny is taller than 90 percent of girls her age. That is, if you took Jenny and lined her up with 100 little girls the same age, Jenny would be taller than 90 of them and shorter than 10 of them.

WEIGHT FOR AGE

We find Jenny's age in years along the scale at the bottom of the chart, and her weight at each age in the Pounds scale along the right-hand side. We draw lines from each set of measurements and find where they intersect. Each time, they intersect at the 90th percentile. This means that all through these years, Jenny weighs more than 90 percent of girls her age. That is, if you took Jenny

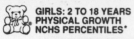

**GIRLS: 2 TO 18 YEARS
PHYSICAL GROWTH
NCHS PERCENTILES***

Name **JENNY**   Record #

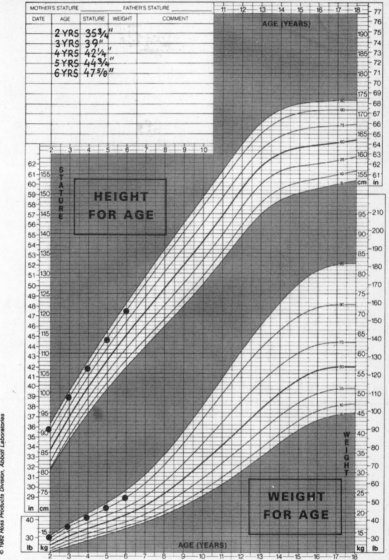

DATE	AGE	STATURE	WEIGHT	COMMENT
	2 YRS	35¾"		
	3 YRS	39"		
	4 YRS	42¼"		
	5 YRS	44¾"		
	6 YRS	47⅝"		

HEIGHT
FOR AGE

WEIGHT
FOR AGE

*Adapted from: Hamill PVV, Drizd TA, Johnson CL, Reed RB, Roche AF, Moore WM: Physical growth: National Center for Health Statistics percentiles. AM J CLIN NUTR 32:607-629, 1979. Data from the National Center for Health Statistics (NCHS). Hyattsville, Maryland.
© 1982 Ross Products Division, Abbott Laboratories

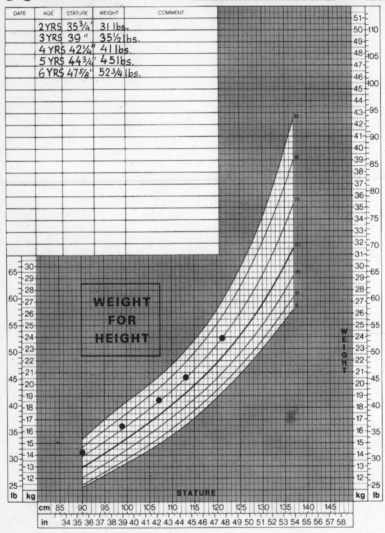

GIRLS: PREPUBESCENT PHYSICAL GROWTH NCHS PERCENTILES*

Name **JENNY**   Record # ____

DATE	AGE	STATURE	WEIGHT	COMMENT
	2 YRS	35¾"	31 lbs.	
	3 YRS	39"	35½ lbs.	
	4 YRS	42¼"	41 lbs.	
	5 YRS	44¾"	45 lbs.	
	6 YRS	47⅝"	52¾ lbs.	

WEIGHT FOR HEIGHT

STATURE

WEIGHT

51214 09893WB
(0.05)/JUNE 1994

LITHO IN USA

and lined her up with 100 little girls the same age, Jenny would weigh more than 90 of them and weigh less than 10 of them.

Therefore, her height for age and her weight for age are both at the 90th percentile. They match. So you'd think that Jenny would weigh exactly the average amount, wouldn't you? That if you lined up Jenny with 100 little girls the same height, 50 of them would weigh more and 50 of them would weigh less?

You might think so, but that is not the case.

This chart doesn't tell us what is an appropriate weight for Jenny. It can't. At any age, some children are tall and are supposed to weigh more; others are short and are supposed to weigh less. The way to get an idea of Jenny's "just right" range is to see what she weighs in relation to her *height,* not her age.

WEIGHT FOR HEIGHT

So we use the Weight for Height chart instead.

We find Jenny's height in inches along the scale at the bottom of the chart, and her weight in pounds along either of the scales at the sides. We draw lines from each and see where they intersect. They do not intersect at the 50th percentile but at the 75th percentile. This means that if you line up Jenny with 100 little girls her height, 75 of them will weigh less than Jenny, and 25 of them will weigh more than Jenny. Jenny is at the top of the "just right" range for height.

This is a perfectly fine weight for heavyset, muscular Jenny.

But for a child of slender build and little muscle, this would be a slightly concerning weight—one that you'd want to keep an eye on. This difference between the two weight charts becomes much more marked after the age of six. After age six, the Weight for Age chart becomes less and less trustworthy, as shown by Jenny's friend Nancy. See the next chart.

Nancy's Growth Charts

Here is what can happen if you trust the Weight for Age chart instead of the Weight for Height chart.

Nancy has always grown along the 50th percentile for height.

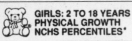

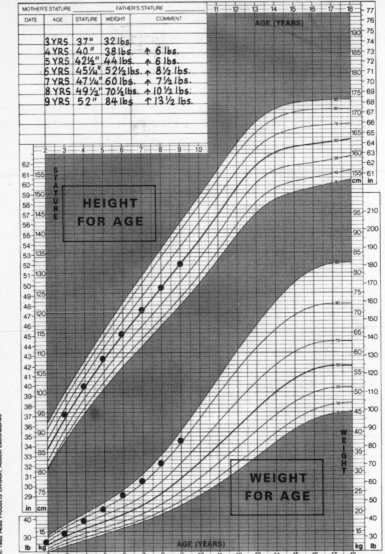

MOTHER'S STATURE		FATHER'S STATURE		
DATE	AGE	STATURE	WEIGHT	COMMENT
	3 YRS	37"	32 lbs	
	4 YRS	40"	38 lbs.	↑ 6 lbs.
	5 YRS	42½"	44 lbs.	↑ 6 lbs.
	6 YRS	45¼"	52½ lbs.	↑ 8½ lbs.
	7 YRS	47¼"	60 lbs.	↑ 7½ lbs.
	8 YRS	49½"	70½ lbs.	↑ 10½ lbs.
	9 YRS	52"	84 lbs	↑ 13½ lbs.

AGE (YEARS)

HEIGHT
FOR AGE

WEIGHT
FOR AGE

STATURE

WEIGHT

AGE (YEARS)

*Adapted from: Hamill PVV, Drizd TA, Johnson CL, Reed RB, Roche AF, Moore WM. Physical growth: National Center for Health Statistics percentiles. AM J CLIN NUTR 32:607-629, 1979. Data from the National Center for Health Statistics (NCHS), Hyattsville, Maryland.

© 1982 Ross Products Division, Abbott Laboratories

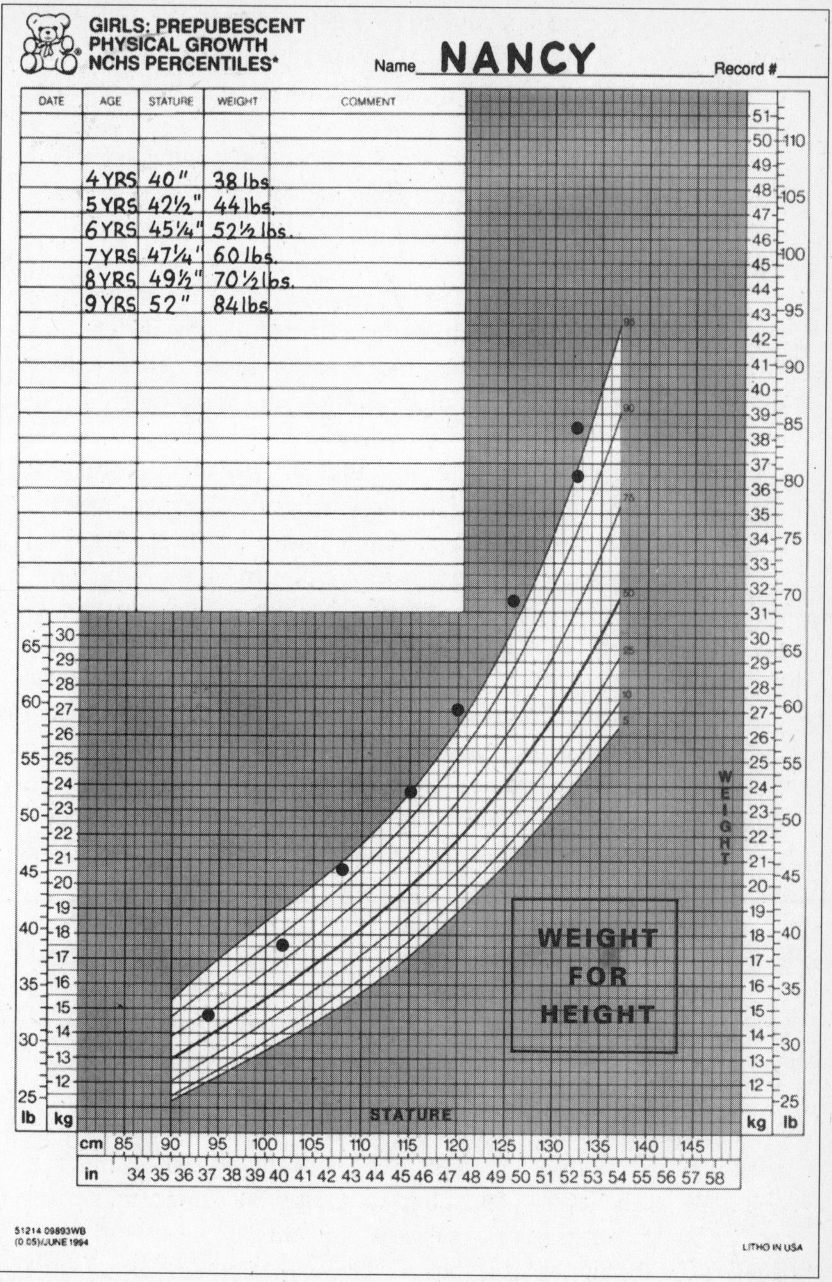

GIRLS: PREPUBESCENT
PHYSICAL GROWTH
NCHS PERCENTILES*

Name **NANCY**

Record #___

DATE	AGE	STATURE	WEIGHT	COMMENT
	4 YRS	40"	38 lbs.	
	5 YRS	42½"	44 lbs.	
	6 YRS	45¼"	52½ lbs.	
	7 YRS	47¼"	60 lbs.	
	8 YRS	49½"	70½ lbs.	
	9 YRS	52"	84 lbs.	

WEIGHT
FOR
HEIGHT

STATURE

WEIGHT

51214 09893WB
(0 05)/JUNE 1994

LITHO IN USA

When she was a preschooler, her weight was also in the 50th percentile on both weight charts: the Weight for Height chart and the Weight for Age chart. During these early years, the charts show the same.

But starting at around age six, Nancy started adding extra fat. However, Nancy's Weight for Age chart shows only a mild increase in chubbiness, whereas the Weight for Height chart shows a much more worrisome situation.

From age four to age six, Nancy's reading on the Weight for Age chart increased from the 50th to the 75th to the 90th percentile. From age six through age nine, there were no more increases: She stayed at the 90th percentile of weight for age. Many parents and physicians feel reassured by this kind of curve. First, the increase was gradual, over two years. Second, the 90th percentile is still "on the chart." Third, her reading on the Weight for Age chart eventually became stable at the 90th percentile, instead of increasing.

But when these same exact figures are plotted on the Weight for Height chart, we see that Nancy's weight is not at all stable on one percentile line. It has soared from the 50th percentile to the 80th, then to the 92nd, then to the 95th percentile—and then becomes progressively farther "off the chart"! When Nancy was seven years old, her weight was one and one-half little boxes above the 95th percentile line. When she was eight years old, her weight was three little boxes above the 95th percentile lines. At nine years, Nancy's weight is four little boxes above the 95th percentile line. Her weight is deviating farther and farther "off the chart."

If we relied on the Weight for Age chart, we might feel that little, if any, intervention was needed for Nancy. If we use the Weight for Height chart, we are alerted to help her out.

Calipers to Measure Body Fat as Opposed to Weight

The use of calipers, a little instrument for measuring skinfold thickness, is another technique. Theoretically, this measures the thickness of the layer of fat a child or adult carries on various parts of the body. Sometimes several measurements are taken and averaged: from the upper arm, the calf, below the shoulder blade, and so on. Most of the time, either the upper arm or under the shoulder blade alone is used.

Then you take the fatfold measurement, put it on a chart, and see how much more fat a child or adult is carrying compared with others of the same sex, age, and state of physical maturity.

You'd think that this would be the ideal way to measure body fat, and sometimes it is. When performed accurately, it does away with the factors of body build and muscle development in deciding how much weight is extra fat.

In expert hands, this works well. But you'd be surprised (or maybe you wouldn't) how often the fold-making and measuring part isn't accurate. You have to mark anatomic landmarks carefully and measure from them accurately. You have to be sure you get no muscle in the fold you are measuring. How much flesh to squeeze? How hard to squeeze it? How do you do it tactfully, without the child's feeling embarrassed and self-conscious?

At any rate, this kind of measurement is not performed routinely, so I do not use it in this book. Nor do I use another kind of chart, the BMI or Body Mass Index chart. The BMI chart is based on height and weight measurements, but it involves calculations in meters and kilograms. It is awkward and has only dubious advantages over the Weight for Height chart. Moreover, it is inaccurate for children less than a meter—about a yard—tall and is mostly used for adolescents and adults.

Once you and your pediatrician have determined that your child is carrying extra weight, how can you help your child slim down?

Your goal is to help your child slow down the rate of weight gain as the child grows in height.

So it is easier to tackle extra chubbiness before, or early into, the school-age years. For one thing, it takes time to grow into extra weight. At the age of seven, for instance, it takes about a year and a half to "grow into" each 20 percent of overweight, even if the child gains absolutely no weight during that year and a half. For another, as parents you have more control over your children's lives when they're little.

Moreover, when a school-age child is overweight, the extra weight can kind of take on a life of its own. From age two to age ten, children normally do not increase the *number* of fat cells they carry. If they gain just a little extra weight during this time, that's fine: The fat cells they already have just fill up a bit.

But if they carry a lot more weight as fat, somehow the extra fat inspires the creation of more new fat cells. Once those surplus cells are born, they are there for life, each little cell clamoring to be filled with fat. All that clamoring seems to make the body feel unhappy and deprived until it reaches a certain, and overly high, weight.

Finally, puberty can be a complicating factor for girls.

Puberty comes sooner than many parents expect and has more implications for weight than most parents realize. Extra weight actually brings on puberty sooner: as early as age eight in girls and as early as age nine in boys. (Ten for girls and eleven for boys is average.)

In girls, the hormones of puberty stimulate new fat cells to form. Moreover, once menstruation begins, at an average of two years after the beginning of puberty, most girls slow down in height growth dramatically and soon stop growing altogether. At that point, they can't "grow into" the weight they have. So weight gain in childhood hastens puberty, and puberty, in turn, initiates more weight gain!

Boys, on the other hand, may well slim down during puberty as testosterone converts fat into muscle. However, you can't count on this.

When you intervene to help your child, what do you tackle first?

It's a good idea to start with an analysis of exercise.

Burning up more calories in exercise and building muscle are safer and more effective ways to slow down weight gain than eliminating calories. Increasing a child's exercise can be tricky, however. The first thing to do is to analyze how much, and what kind, of exercise the child is already getting.

It's easy to think that a child is getting plenty of execise when that is not truly the case. Many preschools devote much of the day to crafts and projects and pre-reading activities. In many day-care centers, children spend a lot of time going along on errands (sitting in cars, waiting in lines), watching TV, or taking rest periods and naps. Even school-age kids may not be very active. Only 36 percent of public schools offer daily physical education classes.

Many kids don't get around under their own steam. They are bused or carpooled.

Even during physical education classes and recess and lunch, many children don't really run around. Gym class can be spent learning the rules of games or playing games of skill rather than ones of activity. Many school-age children use their free time for giggling on the swings or other sedentary activities.

Then there's food.

It's easy to think that a child with normal food intake isn't eating enough. From about a year of age until the growth spurt of puberty, it's normal for a child to eat a good breakfast, a fair lunch, and practically no dinner, with a couple of snacks between meals. This can be hard to take, especially if dinner is the "family meal" and the only one you actually see your child eat or not eat.

Parents and grandparents and day-care providers often describe a child as a good eater or as not a good eater. The problem is that the good eater may in fact be eating more than is truly good and that the child labeled not a good eater may be coaxed and cajoled and seduced and bribed and commanded to eat more than is good.

Many research studies have looked at whether young children can determine on their own how much to eat. Most of these studies support the observation that children eat the right stuff and gain the appropriate amount of weight as fat when their loving adults allow them to decide how much and what to eat. But there are a couple of caveats here.

First, the food offered to the children in the studies was very nutritious. In children over age two, fat calories were kept to under 30 percent of the total calories offered. Nobody gave the kids a choice among brussel sprouts, liver, and chocolate ice cream.

Second, the studies show that young children (preschool and under) choose more wisely when parents don't determine portion size or insist that some foods be eaten and others on the table be reserved for a "reward" as dessert. Chubbier children had parents who *did* intervene, urging one food and restricting another. However, the studies did not consider the possibility that the parents were intervening *because* the children were already chubby—that the intervention was not a cause of but a response to parents' concerns about chubbiness.

Nevertheless, the studies do support what every parent knows: The more fuss you make about food, the more it becomes a power struggle, the more urgently the child defies any rules and restrictions about it.

When it comes to food, parents should have one role and children should have another. Parents should decide what is healthy and tasty and affordable, and buy it. Parents should decide when mealtimes and snacktimes are. (Parents and older children together can construct menus and prepare the food.) Children decide how much, and which, food to eat.

When it comes to overly chubby children, minor changes can make a big difference: scheduling a definite snacktime rather than doling out munchies all day long; changing from whole milk to nonfat or 1%; packing a different lunch for school, for instance. But counting calories and measuring portions are the province of adult dieters, bless their hearts. These methods are not for kids.

A few major changes about food can be very worthwhile, too. It is a parent's perfect right not to purchase sodas and empty-calorie juices, high-fat snacks like potato chips, and gooey sweet snack foods. Eating such foods can be very habit forming, and they contain nothing useful except calories.

Can parents really help a child slow down weight gain on a long-term basis?

Absolutely. I've seen it done, again and again. The trick is to keep in mind that you are helping a child not to lose weight but to grow into the extra weight already there. This means slowing down or even stopping weight gain over a year or two or even three. This means that you make a long-term plan, that you don't get upset at minor deviations, and that you don't expect immediate results. You aren't always measuring and weighing and muttering over the charts. That's a sure-fire recipe for rebellion, discontent, and major distress.

Toddlers and preschoolers are the easiest to help along. They are still living in an environment that you, the parent, design. But it's also possible with kids up until puberty.

It is not the easy path. It's not every parent or family that can do it. But it's not overwhelmingly, agonizingly difficult either.

The primary goal for parents is to help a child of any age feel comfortable making mostly healthy choices—about exercise and diet, yes, but also about managing time, making friends, taking risks, telling the truth, and a million other things.

Growing into the baby fat, maintaining a weight that is in the "just right" range for a particular child, requires parental patience, commitment, involvement, and most of all a sense of proportion. Our primary goal is not to raise a thin child, or even a child who is not overweight: It's to raise a child who feels capable of taking charge of things, and who feels competent, clever, cute, loved, liked, and enjoyed.

That means that we mustn't regard a child's extra weight as The Enemy, or the child as a project. Teasing; sarcasm; nagging; exasperated expressions and sighs; comparing with other, slimmer friends and siblings; and public discussion of any aspect of the issue (even success) won't help and ultimately will backfire.

These actions can even be dangerous. We don't know for sure what drives a child to anorexia nervosa or to bulimia. We know that these disorders are complex, with culture, family behaviors, physiology, and metabolism all playing a role. But we suspect that making a child's or a family's life revolve around food and weight may sometimes help to trigger both of these malignant afflictions.

What if despite using the tools in this book, despite your good intentions, despite your helpful pediatrician, your child does not grow into the extra weight?

Then your child's job, and yours, is to make a friend of that extra weight. There is no reason that the extra weight should stifle a child in a bleak world. On the contrary: Look at the famous women and men who have made of their weight an extraordinary blessing: from opera singers and actors and actresses, to statesmen and stateswomen, to intellectuals, to business tycoons of both sexes, to talk show hosts and inventors and heads of universities and scientists and even, I can vouch for it, pediatricians.

Let that extra ponderosness give your child power and dignity. Use it to advantage. Love every ounce of your kid, and your kid will love every ounce of you.

1

Babies: One to Four Months

ROLY-POLY IS HUNKY-DORY
(Usually, Anyway)

The first month of life is a period of adjustment. Babies start out by losing weight right after birth: up to 10 percent of their birthweight. They should gain back up to birthweight by two weeks of age. But it may take a month for the whole family to settle into any kind of routine. Certainly, the last thing any parent should be concerned about in the first month of life is a baby who is too fat! So don't even think of looking at this chapter, or even at this book, if your baby is under a month old.

A baby's brain grows enormously during this period and requires a full share of calories, fats, protein, vitamins, and minerals. Malnutrition in babyhood can permanently impair brain growth, development, and IQ potential. Nothing is worth taking such a chance. If you think your baby really is way out of the range of normal chubbiness, make sure that you have a pediatrician examine the baby and help you guide any changes in diet. Don't do anything like diluting the formula with extra water, or skimping on the number of feedings, or adding cereal, or letting the baby scream in hunger for long periods.

During the first year of life, don't give a baby honey. Rarely, it carries a spore or germ that can cause a serious and potentially fatal disease called infant botulism.

BABY BABYFAT FACTS

- Most babies gain about an ounce a day during the first six months of life.
- Even very plump young babies should never lose weight or go hungry.
- It's much more important that the baby's brain be well nourished than that the baby be less plump.
- Rarely, extreme plumpness may be the very first sign of low thyroid, so very plump babies should have a blood test done. This is true even if they had thyroid screening in a blood test at birth.
- Almost never do babies under four months of age need solids.
- Apple juice doesn't provide vitamins or minerals unless it is artificially fortified; it is sweet and may be habit forming.

●●●

Ebony really gets into nursing. She throws herself upon the breast. At five weeks, she grasps it in both hands. From under heavy-lidded eyes she gazes dreamily. Gulp! Gulp! Gulp! It's an incredible noise—the kind of noise radio programs used to make quiz games out of. In Ebony's case, guesses as to the source of the noise might include: pouring out champagne, feeding a small but hungry walrus, or marching through a swamp.

"I can't nurse her in public," Kahlea says, rocking gently. "It's not a matter of modesty. Nobody cares about that. It's the noise she makes. It just breaks people up, then I start to laugh, and it breaks her rhythm and she starts to cry."

I quickly bite my lip to stifle a giggle.

Ebony is very round. Her black hair is plastered in round

curls; her cheeks and even her nose are round. If you wanted to stencil a picture of Ebony, you could use quarters and nickels and dimes for the outline.

For her age, Ebony is just right.

Now, some babies this age aren't just round; they're fat. A few are really, really fat. But somehow they don't look distressing the way really, really fat older children may. They just look cute. Should you be alarmed? Should you do anything?

Almost never. Plump or even very fat babies this age are learning something crucial about the universe: that it's a lovely place. They rely on sucking and being held and handled lovingly for this insight. Being deprived, even in a good cause, isn't a good lesson.

Besides, most chubby babies slim down as they become infants and toddlers. They become so entranced with rolling across the room after the dog and crawling under the bed in search of lint particles that they would rather move around than eat.

Even if they don't slim down spontaneously, intervention is much more appropriate later on when they take pleasure from a greater variety of entertainments and have more inner resources.

THE GOAL

The goal for the first few months is to make eating delightful and reciprocal. A baby learns during this time that the world is a welcoming, satisfying, comfortable place. One of the easiest ways to learn that is to discover again and again that when you are hungry you are fed, at your own pace, with something you love, by someone who loves you.

THE CHALLENGE

But every now and then, it's clear to everybody that very plump babies aren't really happy about their plumpness. They're not jolly; they're irritable and grumpy.

If very fat babies don't seem to be enjoying life fully, it's often because they haven't gotten the hang of being hungry, eating to satisfaction, and then being full. They are confused, and the confusion makes them unhappy. They might be confused because they mix up the feeling of being too full with the feeling of hunger. Or the feeling of gas pains with the feeling of hunger. Or the feeling of pooping with the feeling of hunger. Or even the distress of boredom with the feeling of hunger.

But their confusion and unhappiness are nothing compared with the confusion of their parents.

"If he isn't hungry, why does he eat?" "How can she be bored! She's only four months old!" "You can't spoil a baby this age. If she cries for a bottle, she can have a bottle."

There are two reasons to try to remedy such a situation. First, it's too bad when a baby's inner confusion and consequent overfeeding dims the joy of life in this period. After all, being a baby is supposed to be fun. So is being a parent. Second, if there is a strong family history of obesity, having a fat baby may make parents believe that they won't be able to do anything later to keep Cherub from growing into a fat toddler, child, teenager, adult.

When I see a very plump baby who is happy and active and performing all the tasks of the age, I don't worry one single tiny bit. But if I see a baby who is irritable and frantic, or whose life is pretty much devoted to eating to the exclusion of other joys, I suspect that we could intervene to make that baby's life happier. I feel the same way when:

• A very plump bottle-fed baby of normal height demands and gets more than thirty-two ounces a day of formula.
• A very plump nursing baby, over three weeks of age, is still nursing more often than every three or four hours.
• A baby who was "just right" in weight starts to gain very rapidly, shooting up the Weight for Height curves.
• The parents tell me or show me that their lives are chaotic or overly stressed, and that food is the way they make themselves feel better.

• A baby who had been "just right" when cared for at home suddenly starts getting fatter and fatter when put in the care of someone else.

• A baby's parents are worried.

"I know babies are supposed to be plump," says Marissa's father, "but look at her: Her neck is only a theoretical possibility. Personally, I've never seen it. Who knows what's trapped in there? I told Bess we ought to use the vacuum attachment for sofa creases."

"My mother says I was just the same when I was a baby." Debby makes a grimace. "I've been fighting my weight since junior high."

So there are situations in which babies and parents need help: a little detective work, a bit of analysis, a few suggestions.

But first things first.

THE ASSESSMENT

You can tell a lot about a baby this age just by looking.

But it has to be a fairly practiced, impartial, educated look. A baby this age is supposed to be well filled out. A double chin; a round, full belly; padded arms and legs with a crease in the thigh and the upper arm—that's all delightful, normal baby fat.

Truly too-fat babies have *more* than one deep crease in their thighs and upper arms. Their eyes nestle like raisins in their chubby cheeks. Their chub jiggles and may have the dimpled look of cellulite. They might have sprouted an umbilical hernia—a balloonlike protrusion at the navel, pushed out by the large belly. (Do have the pediatrician make sure that this is truly the cause of the hernia; rarely, there is a thyroid or other problem causing it.) If he is a boy, his penis may have "disappeared" into a pad of fat. Don't worry; it's still there.

You can also use the chart for babies this age that tells you what the typical range of weight is for a baby whose sex and length are the same as your baby's.

Usually, you'll be shown this chart at the pediatric office; and

there is one later on in this book, as well. Remember, you don't want the Weight for Age chart; you want the Weight for Length chart. A baby who weighs more than 95 percent of babies of his or her sex and height most likely weighs more than is ideal—even when one takes into account variation in bone structure and muscle mass.

In any event, a visit with the pediatrician will tell you. It will also assure that a very plump baby is plump because of eating a lot, not from other reasons (although usually a baby with hormonal problems causing plumpness has other significant difficulties as well, such as extreme shortness and delayed development). So before you decide that your baby is unusually fat from overfeeding, certainly before you do anything about that fat, check with your pediatrician.

If your pediatrician agrees not only that Cherub is more plump than is desirable but also that this plumpness springs from a feeding problem that is interfering with her and your joy in life, you then need to find out why this is happening. This may take some detective work.

Fat at Birth

Some babies are truly overly plump from the moment they emerge (and clearly have been so for some time in the womb). Often, their mothers are diabetic; sometimes, their mothers are not diabetic but have gained a great deal of weight during pregnancy.

In any event, over these first few months the baby who was fat at birth should not lose weight but should gradually start to grow into the extra weight. Instead of gaining an ounce a day, he or she might gain only two-thirds of an ounce.

Most babies born with extra weight gradually slim down on their own over the first two months of life. If your baby shows no signs of slimming down very gradually during this time, consider whether your baby might fall into one of the following categories. But if he or she is as happy as a clam and is on a reasonable schedule, your pediatrician will probably encourage you simply to enjoy life with such a satisfied customer.

The Topper-Offer

The Topper-Offer is the baby who eats nearly constantly, without ever having enough time to thoroughly digest one meal before chowing down again.

These are usually big, vigorous, nursing babies, who were full term and healthy at birth.

"I'm nursing him every hour and a half around the clock," says Emma, her face emptied of everything but fatigue. "As soon as I finish, Quin starts to scream and scream. I hold off as long as I can, and then I nurse him again. He's nearly five weeks old. If I don't get some sleep, I don't know what I'll do."

Quin, I notice, is gaining a steady two and a half ounces a day, more than double the average weight gain. He has one large and two smaller chins, and both his arms and thighs are deeply and doubly creased. While his belly button was an "inny" at two weeks of age, he now has a fairly good-sized umbilical hernia—the reason, in fact, that his mother has brought him in. His eyes twinkle at me from deep in their surrounding pads of cheek and lids.

Sweet Quin is misreading his internal signals.

• He nurses until his stomach is full and he can't take another gulp.
• As soon as he stops, or even in the midst of eating, he poops. This is caused by a normal new-baby phenomenon: the gastro-colic reflex. As soon as the stomach is full, his rectum automatically empties. And at the same time, his stomach is churning milk into his small intestine. The

whole thing is interpreted by Quin as chaotic, upsetting, and painful.

- "Oh!" he says to himself in nonverbal, primitive newborn fashion. "My stomach hurts. I must be hungry!"
- He nurses, and—Return to step one. Alas!

No wonder everyone in Quin's family has a stomachache.

The treatment here is straightforward.

Once you're sure that this is what is going on (which means running it by your pediatrician!) you embark on a teaching program. Quin needs to learn the difference between the discomfort of too-full and the discomfort of hunger.

Here's what I advise the parents of such babies.

1. First thing in the morning, nurse the baby as usual, or give as much of the bottle as he or she will take.

2. If you're nursing, top off with a bottle of expressed breast milk, just to be sure that the baby is really, really full. (Usually, mothers of Topper-Offers have a few dozen bottles of frozen or refrigerated breast milk on hand. They're nursing so often, their milk production goes full steam, and they have a great deal of surplus.)

3. Then don't nurse again for three hours. This will be difficult. Try giving a pacifier, carrying the baby in a sling, or using a swing; even give a bottle of water with a pinch to a half-teaspoon of sugar in it. But no nursing, no formula. Plan ahead; have someone (preferably very patient and inured to noise) help.

4. If the baby is sleeping at the three-hour mark, don't wake him or her! Let the baby go to four hours, but not beyond. You do want to inculcate a regular schedule. If the baby's awake, feed him or her.

5. At this next feeding, nurse the baby as long as he or she wants or give as much formula as he or she will take.

If the diagnosis of mixed-up sensations was correct, a day or so of this regimen is usually all that is needed to set the baby on the right track. Baby was full; then Baby was comfortable; then Baby was hungry. No longer is he or she just "topping off."

With great gratitude, the baby with this problem will put him- or herself on a regular schedule.

The Crampy, Gassy, Burpy, Overwhelmed Nurser

Some babies swallow an awful lot of air while eating, and this air gives them stomach cramps, which makes them think that they are hungry.

With nursing babies, this is usually because the milk pours out like gangbusters, like a Roman fountain, or Niagara Falls. The hungry baby is confronted with a tidal wave that he or she tries to glug down, snorting and whoofling, as best as he or she can. With the milk, the baby takes in gulp after gulp of air.

Then the same thing happens: "My stomach hurts; I must be hungry." More nursing, more gulping, more cramps, more pseudo-hunger.

To deal with this problem, you can't just stretch out the feedings. You have to deal with this tidal-wave milk letdown.

The following will help:

• Nurse with both mother and baby lying on their sides. This way, the extra flow of milk can dribble freely out of the baby's mouth, and he or she won't have to glug glug glug and work to swallow.
• Nurse on one breast per feeding so that the baby doesn't have to cope with two overwhelming milk letdowns.
• Express a little milk before nursing to reduce the torrent of milk.
• See a lactation specialist. Sometime, pressing on the breast or changing holds or even walking around while nursing will help.

Born to Suck

Some babies are born to suck. You've heard these. They sound like little crickets as they work indefatigably on their pacifiers (or "binkies"), thumbs, parents' thumbs, anything handy. Whether fed by breast or bottle, these babies give every indication that they could suck twenty-four hours a day. It is often very hard to tell whether they are hungry or just want to suck.

"If she's not hungry, she'll leave the bottle (or breast) alone and suck her thumb," advisors say. Not so. The baby doesn't know whether she's hungry or not; what she does know is that she wants to suck—on anything. If the bottle or breast is there, she will suck. She'll gain too much weight, and she'll cry with cramps—which will make her want to suck even more.

A classic vicious cycle.

The solution is to offer the amount of milk that should satisfy a baby of her age and size, and then offer the pacifier in between and after feedings. But sometimes parents are so disgusted with the idea of a pacifier that they can't bear to offer one. Well, you can always help her to find her own thumb.

However, studies show that pacifier use doesn't injure teeth formation unless the "binkie" becomes a habit after six months of age. No studies give any evidence that pacifier use prevents thumb sucking later on. No study shows that early thumb sucking leads to later thumb sucking. In this area, experts are of no help: Parents are on their own.

The True Gourmet (or Gourmand)

Some babies just truly love to eat.

From a very tender age, they radiate bliss while eating, whether bottle- or breast-fed. At around three months of age, they may start to moan with pleasure, or jiggle their foot, or rock themselves; their eyes stare unfocused or half-lidded. A watching adult may experience delight, tenderness, a slight embarrassment, or a sympathetic urge to visit the refrigerator.

These babies do tend to eat too much. They do tend to get fat. And it seems just criminal to deprive them of their deepest pleasure.

Indeed, I wouldn't. I would, however, try to extend this pleasure into other realms. Such babies tend to love sensual touch:

baby massages with lotion, rhythmic swinging and rocking, sucking on different voluptuous items such as pacifiers of different shapes, a very clean adult finger, and hard rubber rings.

Then I'd try to establish a regular and appropriate schedule, rather than feed the baby strictly on demand. Often such a baby, especially a nursing one, loves to snack every hour or two and never turns down the offered breast. But most babies of eleven pounds or more don't have to eat more often than three or even four hours (unless they are very tall and are genuinely pushed to get enough calories to sustain their vertical growth).

Moreover, most average-sized babies can start sleeping longer stretches at night at about eleven pounds. One way to help babies to do this is to help them learn to fall asleep on their own, starting at about two months of age. Not only will this help ensure a good sleep for everyone, but it will also help to delete an unnecessary full feeding in the middle of the night.

But if all this is in vain, and the baby-who-loves-to-eat just gets plumper and plumper, I wouldn't deprive him or her of pleasure. This is the age of learning that the universe is a lovely, delicious, warm, friendly place, and that's more important right now than not getting fat. I would, however, resolve during the coming months to introduce Loves to Eat to a variety of other sensual, exciting, rewarding activities.

THE PLAN

We have three issues to tackle during these early months. First, what kind of milk is best: breast milk or proprietary formula (the brand names) or homemade formula, and why? Second, how can you make sure that the baby is taking the right amount? And third, what about juice and foods?

The Milk

All the milks used for babies this age have the same calorie count: twenty calories per ounce (thirty grams) of milk. So why should one milk differ from another when it comes to weight gain?

It's not just calories that govern nutrition. Breast milk differs from formulas in the kind of fat, protein, electrolytes, and trace elements it provides, and all formulas differ from one another.

NURSING

Nursing gives a potentially too-chubby baby benefits not present in formula. It's not that babies can't become overly chubby by nursing; they most certainly can. But most nursing babies are more slender than ones who are fed formula. Partly this is because a mother's time and milk supply are not inexhaustible. Also, when they offer babies bottles, people tend to get focused on Ounces Taken and Emptying the Bottle. This is not a factor with nursing.

Moreover, the fat that the baby puts on from taking breast milk seems to be of different composition from that gained from formula feedings, and the baby's regulation of fat metabolism is different: The fat is easier to lose.

So if you are able to breast-feed, this is just one more of a huge number of good reasons to do so. (If you want my Ode to Breastfeeding in full, it is in the prenatal chapter of *The Portable Pediatrician for Parents,* HarperCollins, 1994.)

One caveat: It's not a good idea to offer water to a breastfeeding baby. Breast milk contains extra water to satisfy thirst. In fact, nature regulates the amount of water in breast milk so that it varies, increasing when the environment is hot and dry. It's better for the nursing mother to drink the extra water.

FORMULA

If you use formula, you have two basic choices: the proprietary formulas made by the formula companies or the kind you make at home from evaporated milk.

I hope you will choose among the proprietary formulas. The well-known brand names include Enfamil, Similac, SMA, Isomil, Nursoy, Soyalac, Carnation Good Start, and Gerber.

Formula companies have striven valiantly to produce milks whose content in every way mimics that of human milk. The proprietary formulas are better choices for the baby with a risk for overweight than are the formulas based on evaporated milk. Cow's milk, unmodified, is really designed for beings who lead a bovine lifestyle and who need a layer of fat for insulation from the cold and rain. It's ideal for cows.

I am not able to find any study aimed at determining *which* proprietary formulas have a better record at preventing obesity. This is because the focus has been on producing excellent weight gain and achieving no deficiency in nutrition.

So on the obesity score, I don't have any recommendation for one cow's milk–based or soy-based formula over another.

Whichever you use, however, and no matter how chubby or demanding your baby, don't overdilute formula. By this, I mean don't fill half the bottle with regular-strength formula and then add water until it's full, or any other proportion along these lines. Sometimes this strategy occurs to parents as a way to give the baby more volume with no added calories, in an attempt to satisfy what seems to be a huge appetite. Why shouldn't you do this?

- It can be dangerous. Babies can absorb extra water to such a degree that it dilutes the sodium in their blood, and this can cause brain swelling, lethargy, seizures, and, if the condition is severe and left untreated, even death.
- It confirms in the baby the theory that more food is what he or she needs by stretching the stomach capacity.
- It confuses the baby as to the difference between hunger for food and thirst for water. This just adds another confusion about intake for him or her to deal with.

It is far better to give the formula in appropriate amounts and to give water in a bottle between meals if the baby seems thirsty. That is, if the air is dry, if it's hot. If you're extra thirsty because of heat and dryness, she may be, too.

A word of caution: if your chosen formula comes in a high-iron and a low-iron form, get the high-iron one. Iron deficiency in babies can cause permanent developmental and intellectual delay. Finally, if you can't afford proprietary formula, get in touch with the Women, Infants, and Children (WIC) governmental program through your local welfare department.

The Schedule

I believe that parents find it easier to trust babies to eat the right amount if they have some idea of what *is* the right amount, what *are* typical feeding schedules, and why.

NURSING

Many nursing babies are on a schedule by a month of age; and nearly all are *capable* of being on a schedule. Yet many parents, organizations, and books advocate Demand Feeding: nursing the baby whenever, and for as long as, he or she demands it.

Behind this advice is the theory that babies will demand to be fed only when they are hungry and that they will stop eating when they are full.

Indeed, some babies do act in accordance with this theory.

Unfortunately, many of the babies who are at risk for becoming overly chubby do not nurse only when they are hungry and stop when they are full. They nurse when they are startled, or upset, or when they don't have anything to stare at or drool on, or simply when they remember that the breast exists. They nurse and nurse and nurse around the clock, every hour or two.

How can a baby who is nursing to fullness every one to two hours *know* what hunger is?

Sometimes it's not the baby who initiates such frequent feeds; it's the family, and not just the nursing mother. Somebody—mother, father, sibling—is particularly happy to have a baby nurse. It satisfies something deep inside. And why not? A nursing baby gives off a glow: perfectly concentrated, perfectly involved, perfectly satisfied. It's an engrossing and delightful experience in which to participate, even as an observer, even vicariously.

But by a month of age, most babies can be perfectly happy and perfectly nourished on an every three- to four-hour schedule. (Moreover, many babies who weigh at least eleven pounds will be able to give up the middle-of-the-night feeding and may even be able to sleep for eight to ten hours at a stretch. But this depends on how that eleven pounds is distributed. A tall, lanky eleven-pounder needs many more calories to fill out his or her height, so don't push him or her to sleep through the night without a feeding.)

How do you tell if your baby is snacking rather than feeding from hunger?

Here's one way that works well. Pretend that you are bottle feeding. Every time you have the impulse to nurse, or to suggest to the mother that she nurse, pretend that you have to go to the kitchen, sterilize a bottle and nipple, prepare formula, and then wash the bottle afterward. If the baby is really hungry, this will seem like reasonable, appropriate, necessary behavior. If this is just a whim on somebody's part, soothing the baby with another method will seem like the right thing to do.

Here's another. Weigh your baby and have the pediatrician see if the baby's gaining more rapidly than appropriate for body build.

Here's a third: Pay attention to what cues your baby gives you that he or she wants to nurse. Does the baby simply make a motion toward the breast? Does the baby finish staring at the mobile or mouthing the rattle and then look around for something else to do and, not finding it, start to act as if he or she wants to nurse? Or does the baby give clear signs of hunger—unable to be distracted with a toy, wiggles around, looks uncomfortable, and then starts to cry in a way that "means business"?

FORMULA

Most babies do well on about two and one-half ounces a day for every pound of weight. So a twelve-pound baby takes about thirty ounces a day.

And a good rule of thumb for stomach capacity is about one ounce for every two pounds the baby weighs. So our twelve-pounder would do well with a six-ounce bottle five times a day. Because most twelve-pounders can sleep through the night, a good schedule would be to have those five bottles spread out over a sixteen-hour period—that is, one every three hours or so.

However, no baby will eat exactly the same amount every day. One day it's twenty-six ounces, the next day thirty-two ounces.

Most babies this age need no more than thirty-two ounces a day to thrive. I would be a bit suspicious that a baby who routinely, *every single day,* drinks more than thirty-two ounces a day is

Learn to Read the Baby's Signals of Hunger and Fullness

Learning to read the baby's signals of hunger and fullness is a dress rehearsal for the next phase of feeding coming up: baby food. Next month, when you are confronted with a full jar of baby food, an open infant mouth, and a spoon, the temptation will be to try to get the entire contents of the jar into the mouth. It is all too likely to become a game, in which hitting the moving target gives one an unholy feeling of winning. "Hah!" I caught myself shouting in triumph one day over a jar of pureed lima beans.

This is a great time to learn to sense when Cherub wants to eat. With very young infants, stroke the cheek with nipple (human or rubber) and see if Cherub roots toward it and engulfs it. With older infants, see if they bounce at the sight of bared breast or offered bottle, gazing at it with shameless greed.

Then see if the baby consumes the milk in his or her usual style. Gourmet nursers will lick, and pause, and suck, and lick, and pause, and suck but usually won't actually fall asleep on the breast until they are done. Satisfied customers will—metaphorically speaking—tuck in their bibs and nurse without fuss and then stop. Barracudas will latch on, inhale a breastfull or bottlefull, and then thrust it away, gasping and red of face. Once the end point is reached, don't try to coax or force in more.

(A baby who is not thriving will not gain by being coaxed and urged to eat; indeed, this may make matters worse. If your baby is not gaining appropriately, you need medical help promptly.)

Don't Introduce Foods and Juices

FOODS
Why should babies this age need baby food?

They have no teeth, nor the coordination with which to chew. They can't sit up on their own—the position of choice for receiving a spoon in their mouths. They can't tell you efficiently when they want more food, by leaning forward, mouth gaping, and pounding on the high chair. They can't tell you when they've had enough; they're still in that hypnotic love-affair-with-the-parent stage, when they're just likely to go on automatically opening up and swallowing for the pleasure of your smile.

What sustenance would food provide that Cherub doesn't get with breast milk or formula? Ounce for ounce, milk of either kind is far superior nutritionally to food. Food has been shown to impair the absorption of iron from breast milk and formula; and iron, as noted, is a key factor in attaining normal intellectual development, to say nothing of avoiding anemia.

Why is the taking of solid foods considered a rite of passage of babies, an accomplishment that some parents feel denotes sophistication, intelligence, or moral superiority? I have considered this question long and deeply and have come to the conclusion that it is another instance of our love affair with brand names. Once one's baby can eat solid foods, parents can argue forth on the relative merits of Gerber, Beechnut, Carnation, Earth's Best, and the homemade variety. No, no, no. Tell me it is not so.

Babies need several skills before they are ready for solid foods. Most are ready between four and six months of age, so see the following section and hold off until then.

JUICE

Hah! My very favorite scapegoat! I am very angry at juice. Most especially, at apple juice. It is the beverage of choice for the infant, toddler, and preschool set.

Why would a baby this age need juice? Why would a baby of *any* age need juice? Don't look to the juice ads to tell you; they will only describe juice as pure and wholesome. Pure what? Well, not to put too fine a point on it, pure sugar. With some potassium.

Apple juice in its wholesome and pure natural state has insignificant amounts of vitamin C and iron. Most makers of infant apple juice kindly add some of each, and maybe even some calcium, too. Is it then still pure? Wholesome? Necessary?

The ads may point out, of course, that the (added) vitamin C helps babies to absorb the (added) iron. But they don't point out that a breast-fed baby who may need such supplements after four months of age is already having loose stools and that the apple juice may transform them into diarrhea. And they don't point out that a formula-fed baby has all the vitamin C and iron self-contained in the formula.

I wouldn't mind that so much; it's the attitude toward "natural sugar" that I mind. What, pray tell, is "natural sugar"? It is fructose (fruit sugar), which is very readily absorbed and turned into fuel and/or fat. Does your baby need a drink that is pure sugar, albeit natural sugar, with no redeeming characteristics?

I doubt it.

I know of only one problem that demands juice, and that is constipation in a formula-fed baby. *Breast-fed babies do not have constipation.* Breast-fed babies normally have infrequent stools after about a month of age. This is because they have outgrown the automatic reflex that allows them to generate stool without any voluntary effort every time the stomach is full. A breast-fed baby who is gaining weight well may generate stool only every three or four days, or even less often. I remember my little friend Ashton, who pooped every eleven days like clockwork. Well, sort of like clockwork; actually, more like an avalanche. If a breast-fed baby is *not* gaining well and having infrequent stools, the problem is not constipation but either underfeeding or illness.

Constipation in a formula-fed baby means stools that are harder than Play-Doh or soft peanut butter. Normal constipation can occur in formula-fed babies who are healthy and thriving. If a baby is not healthy and thriving, this is not simple constipation: It's a medical problem. Get help.

The solution to normal constipation may be extra water, or it may be a little prune juice. Why prune juice? Not because it's more nutritious than apple juice (it's just slightly more so) but because it is high in fiber and is a natural laxative. Even more important, nobody ever cuts a sweet tooth on prune juice. The prune is a fruit of ridicule, not of patriotism: America never had a Peter Prune Pit, only a Johnny Appleseed. You are in no danger of overusing it.

And when, you ask, *should* you start juices as a beverage? Mercy, after that diatribe? Here's when. Start juices when you want your child to have tooth decay and loose stools, to refuse milk and water because they aren't sweet enough, and when you have some extra money to spend on little straws and cartons to help add to the landfill.

Thank you. I feel much better now.

Leaving Cherub with Others: Grandparents and Day-care Providers, Babysitters and Nannies

Despite the emotional pain suffered by many mothers returning to work when Cherub is this young, there is one big advantage.

You are allowed to be, and indeed are supposed to be, faintly distraught, very picky, highly emotional, and dependent on the advice of your pediatrician—which you follow to the letter.

Take advantage of this now, and it will stand you in good stead later. Write down exactly how you want Cherub fed. Make sure that you observe your Other Mother. Make sure that she is heating the expressed breast milk safely—if in the microwave, that she never heats the nipple, that she allows the milk to cool, mixes it thoroughly to get rid of hot spots, and tests the temperature on the inside of her wrist. Make sure that she is mixing the formula exactly as directed and with very clean instruments. Make sure that she never re-feeds a partially drunk bottle of either: The baby's mouth germs can multiply in the milk and cause illness or the mouth yeast called thrush.

Hover over her to be sure she is alert to the baby's cues for hunger and fullness, that she's not overwhelmed by toddlers and preschoolers or distracted by soap operas—televised, or in her own life.

Make it clear that your particular baby is not to have a sip of juice or a bite of baby food until your pediatrician advises them.

Leave no doubt in her mind that you are the complete authority on your baby's diet.

Of course, at the same time, shower her with admiration and thanks for her loving care and clean habits and the cheerful ambience her presence creates.

The point is that being very scrupulous now will pay off in the next few periods, during which any adult will be tempted to fall into bad feeding habits: coaxing the baby to eat more or more rapidly than he or she wants, giving a juice bottle to produce a little peace and quiet, using little goldfish crackers as rewards or distractions. If you produce a climate of appropriate intimidation now and never let up in your scrupulousness, you will find this a lot easier than correcting lapses once they occur.

Now I know you are thinking: What's this? No snacks for a toddler? No birthday treats? No *fun*? Of course not. All of these are in the cards. But you want to be the judge of how many and what kind of snacks and birthday treats are appropriate, and to keep the focus of fun on activity, not on more and more munchies.

This is the time in which to cut your parental teeth, so to speak, in asserting your authority over how other people care for your baby. Go to it. If you need to, say it's doctor's orders. I ordered it, and I'm a doctor. There.

THE MORAL OF THE STORY

Most babies start out loving to eat. They love it so much it's a miracle they stop to do anything else, like sleep or stare at dust motes or learn to put their hands in their mouths. (In fact, it is my theory that nature had to provide a gimmick to bring a feeding session to a halt: that is, the reflex that makes a baby generate stool when the stomach is full. This astonishing sensation distracts them long enough to stop eating and go to sleep.) The lesson for babies and parents during these four months is a delightful one: making feeding a delicious and rewarding and mutual activity, whether it's by breast or bottle, with no worries right now about gaining too much weight—unless the weight gain is a sign that something is out of kilter. So savor these months. That delight won't disappear as you need to start paying more attention to how much of what your baby eats.

2

Infants: Four to Twelve Months
GODS OF THE FOOD

Even the chubbiest of babies between four and twelve months of age should not lose weight but merely slow down their rate of gain. The brain is still growing at a breathtaking pace, and no worries about controlling chubbiness must get in the way of feeding the brain. Instead, the focus at this point is on helping babies to follow their own instincts when eating. This means not coaxing or forcing or withholding; it means tolerating self-feeding and mess; and it means providing nourishing, appetizing food that doesn't corrupt the infant palate by being overly sweet or salty or fatty. It means not using food as reward or bribe. Fortunately, the whole enterprise can be an awful lot of fun.

Toward the end of this period, exercise becomes a factor. Not just for parents, who will get plenty of it chasing Cherub around the house, but for the baby. Hint: Babies climb before they walk.

Do not give honey to a baby under a year of age; it can cause a rare disease called infant botulism. Also, don't home-cook beets, turnips, carrots, and collard greens, unless you know that they were grown in an area free of nitrates. Once in a blue moon, a baby becomes ill from these substances.

INFANT BABYFAT FACTS

- Most babies gain about an ounce a day for the first six months and about half an ounce a day from six months to a year.
- Even very plump babies shouldn't lose weight but only slow down their rate of gain.
- While only 10 percent of very plump babies go on to become obese as adults, every baby forms important food-related habits and attitudes during this time.
- Until a year of age, babies should drink breast milk or high-iron, brand-name formula—not regular cow's milk or home-made evaporated milk formula.

I shall always remember Thomas, King of Thighs.

When five-month-old Thomas and his rail-thin mother appeared, various staff members would make an excuse to come over and squeeze those delicious pudgy thighs. The whole scene was reminiscent of Charmin toilet paper commercials.

Here is Thomas at nine months. Yes, here is Thomas, but where are his thighs? They are still round and dimpled, but that super-pudge, that squeezable deliciousness, has firmed up considerably. Thomas still jiggles, but not much.

Thomas has slimmed down.

How come? asks my faintly disappointed medical assistant.

Well, Thomas now feeds himself, mostly. He grabs handfuls of semisolid foods, like mashed potatoes and soft-steamed vegetables and pureed meats, and stuffs them into his mouth. Mealtime is no longer a banquet. It's fast food, it's drive-through, it's sustenance only. Food does not occupy his thoughts. What does? The stairs and coffee table, the alluring region under the bed. Books and magazines to tear, balls to roll, and anything with wheels to push solemnly from room to room.

By a year of age, Thomas's weight for height falls in the 50th percentile—quite a drop from the 95th he'd attained at the age of four months.

Thomas's Growth Charts

Thomas has always been a tall boy. His length for age has always been right along the 95th percentile. At any time in Thomas's life, if you lined him up with 100 baby boys the same age, Thomas would have been longer than 95 of them and shorter than 5 of them.

On the Weight for Length chart, Thomas started out at the 75th percentile but rapidly gained so that at two months he was at the 90th percentile and at four and six months at the 95th percentile. If you lined Thomas up with 100 baby boys of his length, he would have weighed more than 95 of them and less than only 5 of them.

Then between six and nine months Thomas started to crawl, and his weight for length dropped to the 75th percentile at nine months. If you had lined Thomas up with 100 baby boys of his length, he would have weighed more than 75 and less than 25 of them.

Then he started to cruise around the furniture, and he slimmed down even more. At a year, his weight for length was at the 50th percentile. If you lined up Thomas with 100 baby boys the same length, he would have weighed more than 50 of them and less than 50 of them.

I just saw Thomas at fifteen months, and he hasn't slimmed down further nor gained back any of his baby fat. He is still really cute.

With Thomas, it looks as if nature just took its course. He grew into the extra weight he was carrying and then continued to gain, more slowly than before, along a normal curve. It sounds easy.

But many fat infants do *not* slim down during this age span. And many who were previously just right for weight begin an inexorable trend through plump and chubby to obese.

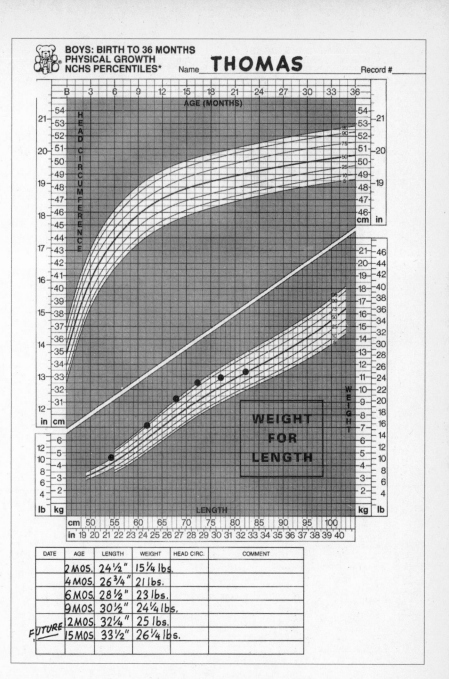

BOYS: BIRTH TO 36 MONTHS
PHYSICAL GROWTH
NCHS PERCENTILES* Name **THOMAS** Record #

DATE	AGE	LENGTH	WEIGHT	HEAD CIRC.	COMMENT
	2 MOS.	24½"	15¼ lbs.		
	4 MOS.	26¾"	21 lbs.		
	6 MOS.	28½"	23 lbs.		
	9 MOS.	30½"	24¼ lbs.		
FUTURE	2 MOS.	32¼"	25 lbs.		
	15 MOS.	33½"	26¼ lbs.		

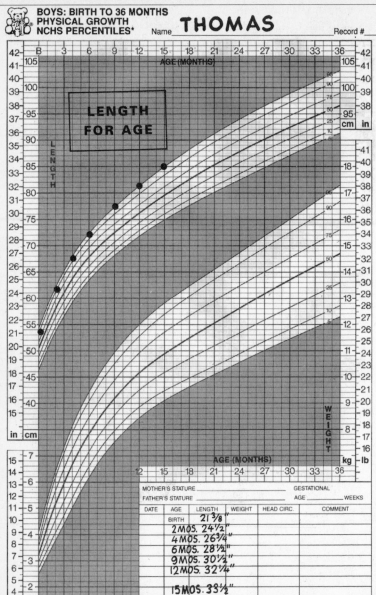

BOYS: BIRTH TO 36 MONTHS
PHYSICAL GROWTH
NCHS PERCENTILES*

Name THOMAS

Record # _____

LENGTH FOR AGE

AGE (MONTHS)

LENGTH

WEIGHT

MOTHER'S STATURE _____
FATHER'S STATURE _____

GESTATIONAL
AGE _____ WEEKS

DATE	AGE	LENGTH	WEIGHT	HEAD CIRC.	COMMENT
	BIRTH	21 ⅜"			
	2 MOS.	24½"			
	4 MOS.	26¾"			
	6 MOS.	28½"			
	9 MOS.	30½"			
	12 MOS.	32¼"			
	15 MOS.	33½"			

*Adapted from: Hamill PVV, Drizd TA, Johnson CL, Reed RB, Roche AF, Moore WM. Physical growth: National Center for Health Statistics percentiles. AM J CLIN NUTR 32:607-629, 1979. Data from the Fels Longitudinal Study, Wright State University School of Medicine, Yellow Springs, Ohio.

© 1982 Ross Products Division, Abbott Laboratories

It's not binging on food that makes most children gain too much weight, nor is it too much TV watching, nor even a genetically sluggish or overefficient fat-making metabolism. It's eating just a few more calories than are worked off in growth and exercise and play, and doing so day after day, week after week, for months and years. This is the age at which this pattern can have its subtle origins.

That's because a whole set of behavioral and eating patterns change during this period and may take parents and caregivers by surprise. Here they are.

• **At between four and six months of age, you'll introduce solid foods and a whole new approach to eating.**
The whole thing needs to be reciprocal and tactful so that eating doesn't become a battlefield or a seductive banquet.

• **Between four and six months, babies perfect the ability to cry not from need but for company and attention.**
Getting the hang of deciphering and responding appropriately is a delightful and crucial task. Both parents and babies need to figure out whether that crying means hunger or a desire to inspect Papa's nose. Most babies also will be ready for solid foods, offered by spoon; ready, that is, to form likes and dislikes, even though milk is still the main source of nutrition.

• **Between six and eight months, babies will be taking food-in-a-spoon more seriously as nutrition, and their amount of breast milk or formula will decrease.**
So will their rate of weight gain, from one ounce a day to about one-half ounce a day (i.e., from two pounds a month to one pound a month). As this happens, the amount of breast milk or formula diminishes. It doesn't make sense to many parents that the amount goes *down* as the baby grows *up*—but it's the way it should be. This is also the age when it first becomes tempting to use food as a distraction, reward, and bribe.

• From eight months to a year, you'll get a true statement of independence.

Cherub wants to and should take over most of the feeding: holding the spoon and sometimes even getting the contents into the right orifice; holding the cup; picking up finger foods like Cheerios, bananas, and potato bugs. At the same time, his range of exploration and mastery just soars: going up the stairs and under the bed; attacking the dog, cat, siblings; figuring out how to drop things into the toilet; opening up and spilling anything—preferably of liquid or powdery form; and taking off his own diaper. And the coup de grace: When you say "No!" about any of this, he'll look at you enchantingly, make sure you're watching, and do it again. No wonder this is the Golden Age of Handouts: little crackers, bananas, apple juice. It may seem to beleaguered caretakers that it's a case of peace at any price.

WHAT HELPS

In general:

• Learn to love spills. Enjoy mess. If you need to, hose everything and everyone down in the shower afterward.
• Keep in mind that you decide what and where and when Cherub eats, and Cherub decides how much.

With planning meals:

• Try to keep meal and snacktimes regular. Nurse or give formula with meals, not spaced between.
• By six months, start to include two or three different kinds of food at a meal: a fruit and cereal, a vegetable and fruit, a vegetable, a fruit, and meat or poultry.
• Steer clear of starchy jarred dinners and pudding desserts.
• Make dessert part of the meal, not something to be earned. Fruit is a good dessert.
• Keep milk (human or iron-fortified formula) the mealtime beverage of choice and plain old water, unflavored by juice,

---

the thirst quencher of choice. (Just as with any new food, babies need to learn to like water, too.) Juice is not a beverage nor a nutritious food: It is a way to treat hard poops or— if you can't manage it otherwise—to give extra iron (if the juice is iron-fortified).

With eating:

• Keep eating confined to mealtimes and snacks (no handouts of munchies; no ever-present bottle of juice or milk).
• If Cherub dislikes a food initially, keep serving it over and over again. Try to project calm acceptance of Cherub's decision. Eventually he'll come to like it.
• Converse pleasantly with Cherub at mealtime about anything that suits your fancy. Don't get too excited about the act of eating; restrain your jubilation when he tastes the rutabaga and your disgust when he inserts a glob of spinach into his nose.
• Avoid hurrying and coaxing, and don't allow anyone to regard Cherub as an empty gas tank that needs to be topped off.
• Encourage Cherub to participate in feeding right from the beginning. Start a cup with breast milk or formula in it at five months, a spoon at about nine months.
• Be alert to when Cherub has had enough. (Who wants to illustrate this one?)

THE GOAL

The more young children can regulate their own food intake, the better. Left to their own devices, they adjust their intake according to exercise and to how much they've eaten at the last meal. The goal now is to keep this in mind, even when sorely tempted to take food decisions out of the babies' sticky little hands.

For babies who are already chubby, the goal is to help them slow down their rate of gain as they become more active. Growth is still so rapid that a chubby baby can grow into the extra weight pretty quickly. No baby this age should actually lose weight, or even stop gaining.

THE CHALLENGE

This is a remarkably delightful period of life for parents and caregivers: something new every day. Feeding is part of all that. It's courtship and pranks; it's messy and sensuous. But there are challenges. The first is not to take Cherub's feeding habits personally. It is the green beans she is rejecting, not you or your work in preparing them. The second is to refrain from using food as reward, bribe, entertainment as much as possible and never to use food, or the withholding of food, as a punishment. This can be very difficult with a highly active climbing, crawling, clinging baby. Third is making sure that the other loving adults who care for Cherub rise to these same challenges.

THE ASSESSMENT

Babies this age are still round. Or, as my Uncle Carl, a Lucky Strike smoker, used to say, "So round, so firm, so fully packed." Double chins are disappearing, but babies this age still will have round, sticking-out tummies and rounded arms and legs with a crease. Their ribs and backbones are well padded.

Up to about six months, babies gain about an ounce a day: two pounds a month. Starting at six months, babies gain about half an ounce a day, or a pound a month: that's about half the rate of the previous six months.

Overly chubby babies, however, have rolls of fat lopping over as they sit, or dimpled cellulite chub; they jiggle. On the Weight for Length chart, they are above the 90th percentile. It is particularly important to use this chart and not the Weight for Age chart. This is because many babies will either accelerate or slow down their growth in length during this time. Of course, when they do so, they should increase or slow down their weight gain as well. If

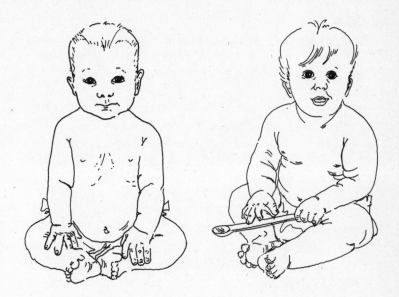

you're using only the Weight for Age chart, this deviation may look worrisome.

Babies change very rapidly in this time, as Thomas demonstrates. Most of the chubbiest babies will slim down as they start to roll, crawl, climb, and cruise around the furniture. But a few will not.

THE PLAN

Each phase of these months rewards its own set of parental skills and baby characteristics, so the plan changes about every two or three months.

Because these are little subsections, each division has its own Goal, Challenge, and Plan.

Four to Six Months of Age: Introducing Solid Foods

THE GOAL

The goal for this two-month period is to introduce Cherub to feeding with a spoon and sipping from a cup, rather than just sucking on breast or bottle; and to make feeding a reciprocal game. He "asks" for a bite or a sip, you produce it, he takes it in at his own pace, then "tells" you if he wants more. So you decide what gets offered, and Cherub decides how much gets ingested at that given meal. Because foods are just taste thrills now, added on to the primary source of nutrition—milk—there shouldn't be any temptation to coax or force or sneak food into that little mouth.

THE CHALLENGE

At about five months of age, babies start to be able to cry for attention, not just out of need (hunger, pain, fear, anger). So answering a baby's cries becomes more reciprocal, too. You listen, trying to feel the tenor of the cry and its urgency. Then you call out, "Daddy's coming." If Cherub stops for a second and seems to wait, that's a good sign that what you heard was an attention cry. As you come closer, you continue to converse. If Cherub is staring in your direction and breaks into a smile as you come close, you've nailed it: That was an attentional cry, and Cherub wants not bottle or breast or close cuddling (though she certainly won't refuse these) but fun and games and conversation.

THE PLAN

What we feed is almost as important as how we feed. Over the next eight months, Cherub needs to discover that all varieties of foods, not just some, are tasty. How foods are introduced may help that discovery along. Meanwhile, more than half the calories come from milk. Having an idea of typical quantities of both solids and milk helps to quench impulses both to overfeed and underfeed.

Milk

From four to six months, foods are just an accompaniment to nursing or bottle feeding, an enticement to let the baby know that there is a world out there of nonmilk foods.

Bottle-fed babies should take twenty-eight to thirty-two ounces of *high-iron* formula daily, and nursing babies should be taking about the same in breast milk, usually five good solid nursings a day. If you are mixing breast and bottle, judging this is tricky. If you are nursing only once or twice a day, you may not have much milk, so count each nursing as about three or four ounces. If you are mostly nursing but giving one bottle every day, count each nursing as six to eight ounces.

These milk requirements can vary a fair amount from one day to the next; what you are looking for is the average intake over three or four days.

The Cup

Now, what does drinking from a cup have to do with gaining just the right amount of weight? Well, a toddler who is still on bottle or breast has a tendency to rely on the soothing, sucking, security-laden, pleasant-memory-enhanced aura of bottle or breast and to seek them for all kinds of reasons other than hunger or thirst.

Babies at around five months of age are ready to experience the cup. They have outgrown the drive just to suck: They now are mouthing, chewing, licking things. Sipping is just another mouth skill. They are more likely to take to the experience now, when they do not suspect an ulterior motive, than later on.

Don't put water or juice in the cup; put in expressed breast milk or formula. This is the message you are trying to communicate: that the vehicle and the liquid don't have to always be linked.

Food

Here are the questions that puzzle the parents I see.

- How can you tell that Cherub is physically ready to eat solids?

• What kind and how much do you offer, and in what sequence, and should you change how much milk you're giving?

• How do you escape the coaxing, urging, battle scenarios over food that most of us remember from childhood and that all of us have witnessed on TV or in the lives of our beleaguered friends?

Before the age of four months, babies are growing so rapidly that they need the most concentratedly nutritious of all foods—and that's breast milk or iron-fortified formula. Right up until six months of age, babies are supposed to gain about an ounce a day (depending on length and gender).

Starting solid foods *before* four months has a lot of drawbacks.

• Many babies have a built-in tongue reflex that pushes the spoon out of the mouth. Even if they accept the spoon, they are so hornswoggled by the experience, or so hypnotically entranced by the game of feeding, that they have trouble telling you when they've had enough. Either they do so by throwing up, or they don't tell you at all and just go on overeating.

• Ah, but why can't you put the food in the bottle and just enlarge the hole? Well, that way the baby has no control over how much solid food he or she eats. The baby just sucks at the milk–food mixture until full. This results usually in a plump baby's becoming fatter and fatter and in a thin baby's becoming skinnier and skinnier. Don't ask me why it happens this way. I think it's some kind of natural law.

• For all babies, solid foods have a highly undesirable side effect: They impair, to a degree, the absorption of iron from breast milk and formula. And iron, I am never tired of harping on, is vital not just to prevent anemia or "low blood" but also for intellectual development and general body growth.

From four to six months, babies are still growing at the rate of an ounce a day, but they're doing a bunch of other things as well:

They are eyeing other people's food with enormous interest, they are outgrowing the urge to suck in favor of the urge to chew, and they are learning the secret of reaching and grabbing. And as everyone knows, one of the main points of reaching and grabbing is reaching and grabbing food.

So at around four months, babies are highly interested in solid foods and remain so for about two months.

If you wait later than six months to start feeding solid foods, you may run into recalcitrance on the part of the baby. I don't know just why, but I have theories. It seems as if during this age a baby decides just what to do with anything that goes in the mouth. Nipples are to suck. Toys and feet are to chew on. Textures are to lick. Crayons are to chew. Cups are to choke on and then to sip from. Cups with spouts are confusing; they can be sipped from or sucked on.

If foods aren't offered during this period, it appears that they fall into a noncategory, with the result that babies don't quite know what to do with them. A baby who is offered only bottle or breast during this period is likely later on to regard the advent of a spoon as a threat or insult. Such a baby may even regard anything but milk as nonfood and won't even reach in and grab a glop and lick it.

So my strong suggestion, and that of most pediatricians and of the American Academy of Pediatrics, is to start solids between four and six months of age.

Readiness

You'll know when Cherub is ready in part because his behavior becomes comical. He'll stare at you as you eat, focusing now on your mouth, now on your hand as it travels from plate to mouth, now on your plate. You may catch Cherub licking his lips as you slurp your soup, looking solemnly intense as you chew your veggies, even making chewing motions as he watches you chew and swallowing when you swallow. You may also have noticed that as the baby grabs and mouths things, not much sucking is going on. He's chewing and drooling, instead. This is nature's way of telling us something.

For nearly all babies, this is likely to happen right at the time that they have made the physical advances that make eating from a spoon possible. They can sit up, propped, without a wobbling head: a good posture to be fed in. They are able to turn away, lips tightly pursed against a probing spoon, when they've had enough. Or to actively eject a bite, usually with accompanying Bronx cheer. Or to regurgitate several stored-up mouthfuls, just to make the point that they were done a while ago and you didn't notice.

The Food Itself

No scientific evidence at all indicates that one sequence of starting foods is superior to another. But there are some intriguing studies about how babies learn to like different foods.

First, babies are born with a preference for sugar. Sugar even can serve as an effective analgesic: Babies who suck on a pacifier dipped in a heavy concentrate of sugar water cry less during painful procedures like circumcisions and blood tests.

If babies are given a choice between a sugary food and any other food, they will choose the sugary food. Reason will not sway them, nor will any number of stories about the choo-choo train carrying the little green Pea Brothers into the railroad station (their mouths).

They also like bland foods that slide down without effort.

The foods that most babies do like, then, are sweetish ones that present little or no trouble: foods like rice cereal, bananas, and yellow veggies like sweet potatoes and squash.

Because it is pleasant to have one's first efforts at feeding crowned with success, most books, grandparents, and pediatricians suggest starting out with rice cereal as a first food.

So how, one asks, will a baby learn to love, say, green beans?

We know but two things about green vegetables. The first is that most babies prefer any of the above-mentioned foods to any green vegetables. The second is that if you serve the green vegetable repeatedly, consistently, over about ten to fourteen days, the baby will go from manifesting dislike to tolerating to active liking.

Putting all this together, here are my suggestions:

• Start with a green vegetable. Give it by spoon. Offer it three times a day until the baby comes to like it. This may take more than a week, but you're in no big rush. And you have several things working for you. First, the baby doesn't know about rice cereal and bananas and sweet potatoes; he or she knows only that what comes from a spoon is green beans. Second, he or she has an innate need and curiosity to eat a solid food. Even if that solid food is not sugary, the baby is still interested.

• Once the baby likes green beans or whatever other green vegetable, add a second food. If you want to be absolutely secure in the green vegetable realm, make it yet another green vegetable. Otherwise, let it be a not-very-sweet yellow vegetable, like carrots or squash. Continue to give the green vegetable(s) the baby already likes, as well.

• Then, every four or five days, add a food from a different food group. As you do, you can construct mini-meals along conventional lines, if you want: fruit and cereal for breakfast, vegetable for lunch, vegetable and fruit for dinner.

• Use pure foods, not "dinners." Read the label of a "dinner" sometime. It is likely to contain water as one of its first and major ingredients, plus a lot of starch, which tells you right away that it costs more than the ingredients warrant. Also, "dinners" tend to contain exotic ingredients like pinapple juice, which your baby probably hasn't encountered, and to which he or she may have a strange reaction, like a mysterious diaper rash. If your baby gets any kind of rash or stomach ache or diarrhea after such a mixed dish, you won't know what ingredient to suspect.

• Wait on meats. For several reasons.

Even lean meats contain considerable amounts of fat. Now, first, Cherub is getting "designer fats" from breast milk and formula, and that's all he needs now. Moreover, unless you are getting very special meats from organically raised animals, you get small amounts of antibiotics, hormones, and other contaminants in that fat. It's not dangerous in tiny quantities, but why have any at all if they are not needed?

This generation of children probably won't be advised, or be able to afford, or live in a world that can condone, the eating of much meat: for reasons ranging from fat intake to the expense of using land for grazing. Why cultivate a taste that may later have to be suppressed?

• Skip the desserts. We know that babies love sugar; you don't have to lure them to learn to enjoy it. Babies this age don't need a food as a reward. Because they have no concept yet of following rules, of good behavior and bad, such attempts are wasted on them. Moreover, baby desserts are something of a rip-off. Check the labels of the dessert jars: They have the same problems as the "dinners." The primary ingredients are usually cheapies like water and starch. Often there is sugar added. Finally, they tend to contain mysterious other ingredients. Don't complicate life. Your baby's best treat is still your shining, pleased, proud face.

During this two-month period, most babies need between about 600 and 800 calories a day total. Their milk intake (32 ounces of breast milk or formula) gives them 640 calories a day. So the average four- to six-month-old needs anywhere from zero calories to about 160 calories from food.

Most jars of baby food for babies this age are four ounces and contain from fifty to seventy calories per jar. (An exception is meat; it comes in two-and-one-half-ounce jars, at about seventy or eighty calories a throw.)

Many smaller babies this age will want only a tablespoon or two three times a day; the larger older ones may need a whole jar three or four times a day.

If your baby (who is already taking thirty-two ounces of breast milk or formula daily) demands and gets more than five ounces of baby food a meal on a regular basis, he or she is either tall or "big all over" or is getting chubby because of too many calories.

Breast-fed babies may need an iron supplement now, usually an iron drop. Some pediatricians also like to include vitamin C and vitamin D as well. Ask your pediatrician.

THE MORAL OF THE STORY

From four to six months, if all goes well, Cherub learns that eating—as opposed to drinking milk—is delightful; that the food which appears in that spoon is neither overwhelmingly sweet nor salty but has distinctive flavors; and that Cherub decides how much to eat, and when to stop. Nobody coaxes or scolds or weeps or gnashes their teeth or puts on a big show.

●●●

Six to Eight Months of Age: The Launchpad

THE GOAL

The goal for the period between six and eight months is to form habits for the future. This is the time when babies start to take over some of their own feeding and to be less agreeable about being fed. Avoiding food battles now can set a good stage for the next phase. That's when it becomes very tempting indeed to use food as a diversion, delaying tactic, bribe, reward, punishment, or substitute for attention and activity.

THE CHALLENGE

That period we've just passed, from four to six months, is such a delightful and tranquil one for many families that this next period comes as a jolt. It's kind of tempting to think of these new impulses on Cherub's part—to pull the cat's tail, roll across the room and eat your latest *Reader's Digest,* bang with the spoon, dump the dish of peas on the floor—as aberrations rather than as developmental advances.

Perhaps, one thinks, if I firmly take control of feeding, if I am in charge of every bite, perhaps he will forget the idea of scooping up handfuls of beets, or of grabbing that spoon and

splatting it in the applesauce. Perhaps that way, too, I can get him to eat vegetables and meat: He just can't stand anything green or brown at this point, and something must be done.

Perhaps if I get him fascinating activity games, he will stop pinching his two-year-old brother: Well, that didn't work; but maybe a handful of Cheerios will distract him until Two can make a getaway.

Perhaps a bottle will settle her down in her car seat. Formula is too rich; apple juice is wholesome and pure and better, and besides, I'll dilute it with some water.

And a bottle is so much easier than a cup: He can hold it himself. Let's postpone the cup for a few months. It's such a mess.

Alas, such theories backfire mightily. Over the next few months, Cherub will foil every such attempt.

Forcing him to let you feed him will turn mealtime into a battle, and one in which only Cherub will win. After all, you can't force a spoonful into his mouth (unless you hold his nose and shove it in, in which case you will receive it right back in your face), nor can you make him swallow. He is likely to dig in his heels and not eat anything you want him to; he'll take up nursing or the bottle exclusively and produce extraordinary noises, from whines to screams, if you refuse him.

Once mealtime becomes a battle, everything else does, too. And right at the time when babies learn how to test limits. The whole concept of a limit on behavior is fascinating, and most babies this age have to take a lot of time and many trials to prove to themselves just what it means. You have to say "No" firmly and move them from whatever it is again and again and again and again. Warnings ("That's no-no, don't touch!") and threats ("If Petey pulls the kitty's tail, Petey will have to go into his crib!") only fuel Cherub's need to discover what will really happen if he persists.

The fewer unnecessary battles, the better. Once the concept of limits is learned, babies seem happier and calmer and more accepting of the limits themselves. So eliminate any battles over biological activities that only babies can control—eating being the main one, now.

Because the whole concept of limits and battles intertwines feeding with everything else, you'll make mealtime happier if you also make Cherub's play environment as interesting and as limit-free as possible. Babies who are told "No!" and moved or punished at every turn are going to turn feeding into a battle on their own, even if you don't—because it's one in which they can count on winning and on getting a lot of attention for doing so.

Another hint: Many toys billed for babies this age are actually boring to them. This includes most activity boards and stuffed animals. A very safe "Exersaucer" or, under **fastidious** supervision, a walker are great—but accidents must be avoided. Safe items that do things when you shake or move or pull them and that can also be mouthed are good. Balls of all sizes are a big hit with many babies.

THE PLAN

As babies move into self-feeding, we want to use that incentive to get them to like foods that are good for them. That means not overdoing the sweets and conducting a tactful campaign in favor of vegetables.

Milk

Breast milk and high-iron formula are the milks of choice. Low-iron formula and cow's milk can lead to iron deficiency and to impaired brain development and to anemia. These milks should be used only if you just can't use the high-iron formulas. If you must use these iron-poor milks, be sure to give iron supplements. Discuss this with your pediatrician and have Cherub undergo a blood test if so advised.

The amount needed of either kind of milk gradually goes down now; an average of twenty-four ounces a day is about right for most babies who are eating solids. If you are breastfeeding solely, most babies can make do with four or five nursings. If you are nursing only once or twice a day, Cherub probably isn't getting that much at that one feeding, so don't be surprised if you are giving more formula.

If Cherub seems to "demand" more than thirty-two or more ounces a day of formula all the way through this period, either he's very tall, or quite chubby, or refusing solid foods, or quite active. Allow your pediatrician to help you figure out which—and what, if anything to do about it.

Some of the breast milk or formula should be given in a cup; a few babies will start making an attempt to help hold the cup at this age. I still wouldn't use a spouted top; it's confusing—should you suck or sip from that spout? You're teaching a skill, not just avoiding a mess. Hah. Easy for me to say. Here, use my scarf as a dropcloth.

Food

Finger Foods

Once Cherub can sit up on his own, leaving his hands free, you can try finger foods.

He is old enough to gum things and make them squishy, but he can't *chew* yet. Chewing, with or without molars, is a rotary motion, not up-and-down. He'll be eight months old or so before he can accomplish this.

He is very vulnerable to choking. He has little idea of what is too big to put into his mouth or to try to swallow.

These are finger foods, not treats or snacks; they are parts of meals that you serve in a different way. He doesn't need salty, sweet, or fatty foods. The mere act of picking up something, gumming it, and choosing whether to swallow or regurgitate is plenty of entertainment.

Regular Meals

Food fills up what the milk doesn't. Most babies this age eat about four ounces of baby food three or four times a day. This can vary wildly from meal to meal and from day to day. The baby's job is to decide how much of each offered food to eat, and the more that decision is left to the baby, the better.

The parent's job is to supply a variety of nutritious foods. These foods should have a soft, lumpy texture, so that gumming them is fun; babies this age possess neither molars nor the grinding motion needed to crunch up real lumps.

It's not a great idea to offer table food to a baby this young. Choking is a big problem. So are food intolerances and allergies. If you do offer People Food, make it bland and soft.

Either get the single-food jarred meals or make the foods yourself. (If you cook your own, remember the warning at the beginning of the chapter.) In either case, the foods should be free of added salt, sugar, and fats. But you certainly can use herbs and spices: a bit of dill, oregano, even garlic, or whatever. No hot sauce, though.

• Let Cherub take the lead. Be alert to when Cherub wants a bite. Before filling the spoon and sitting there, poised and waiting, let him gum and swallow and think about it and turn to you ready for another. Don't encourage gobbling.
• Be alert to when Cherub is all full. Some babies will dump the whole tray; some will turn aside with clamped lips; some will make active efforts to slide out of or tip over the high chair; some will sit there with an unswallowed bite for many minutes and then, thoughtfully, let it dribble down the chin.

The staples of solid foods at this age are vegetables, cereals, fruits, and meats.

But don't lump all vegetables together as a category.

Vegetables
For the purposes of baby feeding, I like to think of four categories of veggies.

1. Those that babies don't start out liking much. These include green peas, beans, lima beans, beets, and spinach.
2. Those that they love: squash, sweet potatoes, and carrots.
3. Those that are very highly nutritious, but too stringy

or otherwise hard to make into a puree: broccoli, cabbage, brussel sprouts, asparagus, and corn.

4. Those that contain carotene. Carotene is a vitamin A relative that, when eaten to excess, turns the skin yellow-orange. This is called carotenemia. You can tell it is not jaundice because in jaundice the whites of the eyes turn yellow, and in carotenemia they stay clear. Carotenemic veggies include all the yellow ones plus spinach.

This organization allows us to confront three challenges.

• How can you get babies to like foods they don't take to immediately?
• How can you set it up so that they will take to those highly nutritious but unpopular vegetables in Group III later in life?
• Should you limit the carotenemic veggies they love, and, if so, why and how?

The answer to the first two questions is one and the same. That is, consistently offer attractively prepared small amounts of the green veggies they *can* have. Don't coax or urge or express disappointment when the veggies are rejected. And start modeling eating those same veggies yourself. This will become even more important in the next few months.

Carotenemic veggies are very nutritious. Cherub's yellow-orange skin color can be rather startling, but it's not a dangerous condition. Or almost never. Here's what to remember:

• Rarely, carotenemia can signify an underlying medical problem. If Cherub is not growing or developing normally or has symptoms such as vomiting, seizures, or poor weight gain, the carotenemia could be another warning flag that something needs urgent attention.
• More often, carotenemia can be a fairly innocent flag that Cherub's diet is out of balance. I know somebody who was permitted a diet of sweet potatoes and carrots to the exclu-

sion of everything else. This is not appropriate. Boy, was he orange. And constipated.

Cereals

What do you want from a cereal? A nice bland texture, iron fortification, and a lack of allergy or food intolerance potential.

The classic baby cereals that fit this description are rice cereal, oatmeal, and barley. Wheat can give several undesirable reactions.

Whichever cereal you give, make sure it is fortified with iron—and consider giving the cereal mixed with apple juice that has been fortified with vitamin C.

Yes, I have not withdrawn my diatribe against apple juice as a beverage; I stick to that. But the iron in the cereal is best absorbed when given with vitamin C. A bit of sweetness in the cereal is not that bad a trade-off.

Baby cereal is highly refined and low in fiber, so it tends to be constipating; it is a traditional food to help diarrhea. The classic combination of cereal and banana tends to be even more constipating.

Once a day is enough for cereal.

Fruits

Fruits are delicious and wholesome and good for you, but the usual baby fruits are not as nutritious as we'd like to think they are. These include applesauce, pears, plums, and peaches. They contain some vitamin C and some traces of other good stuff, like iron and magnesium, but you'd have to eat an awful lot of fruit to get even a quarter of your daily requirement of anything except potassium.

Mostly, fruits are good sources of fiber and good exercise and pleasure for the mouth. Bananas and applesauce help one recuperate after diarrhea.

Citrus fruits are so acidy that they can give diaper and face rashes, and many pediatricians don't recommend them until after a year of age. These include oranges, grapefruit, lemons, limes, tomatoes, strawberries, and pineapple.

Meats

There is no denying that meats are rich in iron, and that the iron in meat is better absorbed than is iron from vegetables, fortified cereals, fortified formula, or even breast milk.

There is also no denying that many babies detest the grainy texture of baby-food meats. Or that meat contains considerable fat: About twenty calories out of seventy in a two-and-one-half-ounce jar of baby meat comes from fat. Or that many people worry about contaminants in meats: pesticides, hormones, and (not to put too fine a point on it) dirt.

If you choose to give Cherub meat now, consider your reasons. Perfectly valid ones include wishing to maintain a family or community culture that loves meat; concerns about iron and B vitamins and trace elements and minerals; and a feeling that meat is getting an unfair bad press.

However, do give a thought to the future. No matter how lean the meat, it is more fat than vegetables and cereals. And starting at age two, we are advised by the American Heart Association and the American Academy of Pediatrics to start limiting babies' fat intake just as adults do. Also, meat is calorie rich: A four-ounce jar of baby vegetable or cereal or fruit runs about fifty calories; a two-and-one-half-ounce jar of meat or turkey or chicken runs seventy to ninety calories. Will you be cultivating a taste for a food that Cherub may have to learn to reject later on?

As for the ecological and ethical concerns about meat, I leave them to others to elucidate.

THE MORAL OF THE STORY

This is a crucial period for the chubbiness issue for two reasons.

First, Cherub is highly dependent on loving adults to make self-feeding the autonomous, sane enterprise it should be, rather than a power play or a realm in which love and food are given or withheld together.

Second, it is an opportunity for loving adults to start to design the environment for the next stage, in which it will be very tempting to curb Cherub's invasive activities and exhausting behaviors by staving them off with food treats.

Eight Months to Twelve Months of Age: Full Speed Ahead

THE GOAL

The goal for the period between eight and twelve months harkens back to the last. Food is inextricably intertwined now with autonomy—that is, the delightful ability to set a goal for oneself and attain it. Every effort you make to keep food food, rather than a bribe, reward, punishment, distraction, peacekeeping device, silencer, or weapon will help to steer or keep Cherub on the "just right" track.

THE CHALLENGE

This age marks the start of feeding problems for many children with a tendency toward chubbiness.

Here's Thomas again. He's not walking yet, but so far this morning (and it's only 9:30, his mother, Julie, reminds me) he has attempted to crawl up the stairs twenty-seven times, only to be foiled by the gate at the third step, only to yell for help, only to be rescued and carried back down to the playroom. (The base of the staircase is too wide for the gate to be placed at the foot.)

He has made his two-year-old sister run screaming to her mother, having bitten her toes, pulled her hair, and pinched her— "He plucks up just a tiny little piece of skin and then pinches and twists at the same time, and then he laughs"—on four occasions. He has explored the cat's anatomy, and no one can find her. The red crayon and the green crayon have been rescued, half-chewed, from his mouth; a geranium flower and, Julie fears, part of a snail have made it down the hatch.

Now Thomas holds onto the couch with one hand and performs the squatting dance and Uh Uh noise that mean he wants his music video turned on. He reinforces this desire by finding the remote and pushing all the buttons. Fortunately, a program on the Japanese stock market (in Japanese) comes on and Thomas shuts up and watches, after one crow of utter delight.

"It certainly isn't a medical emergency," Julie apologizes, "but

I'm at my wits' end. I hate to think of him getting so fat again, but I find myself doling out Cheerios and animal crackers just to get a bit of a respite."

Sometimes a multitude of circumstances combine to encourage extra plumpness in babies this age.

It's the age of testing limits, and food helps parents keep their sanity.

Eight- to twelve-month-olds need to learn and practice testing limits. This activity is a developmental milestone. Think of it as an achievement that Cherub is polishing— like pulling to stand and sitting down again, turning jargon into words, opening and shutting a door to figure out appearance and disappearance.

This is a very sweet interpretation, but the fact remains that such repeated testing can drive parents bonkers.

One of the foolproof ways of distracting a limit-testing infant or toddler is to offer tidbits of food. This works not because Cherub is hungry; it's because food has many play aspects: How do you pick it up? Will it crumble or break? What happens to it when it is subjected to saliva? To teeth? When you spit it out? Smear it?

Alas, giving food is also a powerful reward for any behavior. So, soon there is a vicious cycle. Thomas starts toward the cat with fist upraised and jaws in the shark position. Julie dashes up, grabs him, says "No biting! Here, bite an animal cracker instead!" and Thomas understands the lesson clearly: biting will be rewarded with a delightful cookie. Soon, Thomas's family will have to buy animal crackers in bulk sizes.

Food is also a quieter-downer.

Babies this age, especially those with older siblings or in day care, tend to spend an enormous amount of time waiting. They wait for car pools to arrive, during drives to places, at traffic lights, in grocery carts, in waiting rooms.

This is not the activity they were designed for. Yet what to do? Driving a car with a rambunctious screaming ten-month-old down I-5 is asking for a fatal accident. So out come more Cheerios, apple juice, or whatever you find in the bottom of your handbag.

The forces of culture become more powerful, especially TV and parenting magazines.

When you see babies this age eating on TV programs, it is rarely because they are hungry. It is on a whim, or as a treat, or to keep them occupied. Check this out the next time you watch. And watch what the babies are depicted eating and drinking: crackers and cookies and juice, oh my!

Finally, most subscriptions to parenting magazines go to parents of babies in the very young age groups. Look at the ads in these magazines. Here is a rundown in one of them: M&M's, Jiff peanut butter, Tyson chicken patties fried on a sesame-seed bun; Reese's peanut butter puffs; Wishbone salad dressing; Cheerios for snacking; mozzarella cheese for pizza; Bisquick for pancakes; M&M's again; Cool Whip; Quaker Oatmeal; Del Monte Snack Cups; Hershey's Kisses; Miracle Whip Salad Dressing; Duncan Hines chocolate chip cookie and fudgy brownie mixes; Hershey's miniatures; Crisco with a chocolate chip cookie recipe, and Kudos granola bar with chocolate chips or chunks.

You want to ask the Quaker people, What's a nice oatmeal like you doing in a buffet like this?

It's the age when children are given People Food rather than baby food. Often somebody shopped for and prepared that food and likes it when the family appreciates it.

It's not so much that parents feel rejected when a baby doesn't eat something, though this happens. It's that it feels good when a child clearly loves something you've made, and you miss it when that doesn't happen.

Culture also comes into play here. Many family food traditions include fried foods, butter on everything (my grand-mother liked to spread it on radishes and bananas, as well as the usual viands), and desserts with every dinner.

By this age, most children spend some of their time in day care. And in many day-care situations, snacks aren't just scheduled twice a day; handouts also are doled out freely.

Compounding this, there's often a lot of "waiting time" for children in day care: in car pools, waiting for adults to organize things, in various waiting rooms as the day-care parent runs errands. That waiting time is often passed with the help of little bags of nibbles and containers of juice.

Parents of children this age need their exercise and often include the children. But it's the parents who get the exertion, not the infants.

Riding in a backpack or a jogger or on the back of a bicycle isn't exercise. Carrying the backpack, pushing the jogger, pumping the bicycle is terrific exercise.

Temperament starts to play an even more important role than it did earlier.

Some babies, like Thomas, are full of kinetic energy. Others, like Millie, are perfectly content to sit and watch and play with toys that challenge her hands and mind. When the snacks and the handouts are doled out, Millie is perfectly happy to partake. But unless there is an adult who makes it his or her business to get Millie more active, she is likely to sit there, comfortably munching and putting things into things, for hours. When naptime comes, she will sweetly doze off. Left to her own, a Millie can balloon considerably during these months.

Finally, so many babies this age are chubby that we get used to seeing chubby children. Then a "just right" baby tends to look slender, and a slender baby downright skinny.

This phenomenon can fool everybody, even pediatricians, but especially first-time parents, grandparents, and inexperienced day-care staff.

A baby this age is rounded and has a belly that sticks out, but not a double chin or deep creases in thighs or arms. Fat rolls and dimpled fat are not age appropriate. Babies this age are supposed to gain about half an ounce a day, or a pound a month. If they have been overly chubby up until now, this weight gain should be lower than a pound a month, maybe only four ounces a month; ask your pediatrician. Remember: No baby, no matter how fat, should lose weight during this time.

THE PLAN

We are entering the gateway to the world of toddlers: exploring, setting limits, independence. And this all sets the stage for healthy growth later on.

Exercise

For the first time, exercise takes its place as the first part of The Plan to keep a baby in the just right range of weight.

About one-third of Cherub's waking day ought to be devoted to exploring and learning new physical abilities, like cruising and climbing and stooping and starting to walk; about one-third to mastering tasks, such as putting things into things, turning pages, learning the names of things (though not saying them); and about one-third to relating to his beloved adults. To keep this last occupation to one-third and have it not be overwhelming—full of "No's!" and rescues and hovering—Cherub's daily playing field needs to be safe and challenging. This also means that Cherub shouldn't be asked to perform socially far in advance of what is possible: that is, to share, to play interactively with others, to be, in a word, civilized.

Babies this age enjoy a wide variety of skills. Some roll, some creep, some crawl. Most will begin to pull to a stand and cruise around the furniture. Some will start to walk, though the average age for walking is twelve-and-one-half months. Even before they walk, most will climb: up the steps, up the coffee table, even up the couch. Babies with slightly older siblings like to wrestle.

There's also a wide variety of temperaments, though. Some babies are constantly active, and some need outside stimulation, encouragement, even coaxing. This is very worthwhile. The more babies learn to enjoy active play started by others, the more likely they are to initiate it themselves.

Keep an eye on how active Cherub tends to be. The Thomases of the world do not need to be tamed but enjoyed; the Millies need to be stimulated. Millie might take to a low-center-of-gravity toy she can sit on and scoot about on; she might like games of Chase as she crawls and you pursue; she might like to cruise around the sofa playing peek-a-boo. Certainly she might like to explore out of doors—not being pushed in a stroller, but crawling on the beach or grass, if you have safe areas near you. Splashing in a wading pool, under fastidiously close supervision, is fun and can be quite a lot of exercise. Swimming is not recommended (by the American Academy of Pediatrics) until age three because of safety concerns.

If Cherub is in day care, it also pays off to be sure that it is one that encourages activity. Sitting all day in a walker or a playpen so as not to be underfoot isn't much exercise. Nor is sitting in a car seat while someone runs errands.

Parents need exercise too. Just a reminder: A baby in a jogger or a backpack is getting fresh air and entertainment, but not any activity.

Milk

Babies this age should be drinking an average of 24 ounces of breast milk or iron-fortified formula a day, which gives them about 480 calories. Most pediatricians accept the guidelines of the American Academy of Pediatrics: Don't give regular whole milk until a year of age. That's because of concern partly about iron deficiency, partly because of allergy potential, and partly because of suspicions that early exposure to cow's milk may help to trigger juvenile onset diabetes in a small number of children.

As for juice, see the previous sections. To summarize, water is the best beverage for thirst and between meals.

Food

Meals

That leaves about 250 to 400 calories a day for meals. So it's no wonder that a doting adult can worry that Cherub "doesn't eat a thing." It certainly may look as if this is the case.

Prepared "junior" food for toddlers this age comes as six-ounce jars of veggies or "dinners," each of which is about 120 calories. If your average-sized Cherub is drinking 24 ounces a day, he has left in his diet room for only two such jars, that is, four ounces a meal! If he is larger, three jars, or six ounces a meal!

What if you are making foods at home? Then aim at a total of twelve to eighteen ounces of food for a whole day, depending on Cherub's size and snacking habits, and offer from four to six ounces at each of three meals.

THE FINICKY EATER

Finicky eaters are babies who refuse, adamantly, anything but a certain sparse selection of foods. If you are lucky, the accepted foods will be weird but nutritious. For example, Jorge would take only lima beans, prunes, and a special barley cereal from a health food store.

More likely, Cherub will refuse anything except for canned ravioli and fruit cocktail, or a similar combination.

It is easy for weary parents just to give in and produce the same meal night after night until, mysteriously, Cherub refuses to eat it and demands only, say, meat loaf and peaches.

The handling of the picky eater is tricky. Your first concern is not to make food a battle; your second concern is to encourage a variety of nutritious foods; and your third concern is not to give extra calories to a baby at risk for overweight.

What works best for everybody is to make a plate with very small portions of the foods you would like Cherub to eat: a green veggie, a yellow veggie, a fruit, maybe a small amount of meat or chicken or turkey. Then leave Cherub to it. Sit with him for cheerful company, but don't express sympathy or anger or pity or disgust or laughter at his response. Just smile nicely and take him down when he is done. If Cherub is drinking his twenty-four ounces of milk a day and eating breakfast or lunch, he will not starve even if he is not eating his nutritious dinner. After a week or so of this, I guarantee that Cherub will start tasting what is on the plate.

THE MORAL OF THE (WHOLE) STORY

Being just right in weight at a year of age augurs well for the future, especially in the baby at risk for being chubby. It usually means that Cherub's parents have been sensitive to the relationship between autonomy and eating and between feelings and food. It means that they have provided a daily environment in which Cherub can concentrate on exploring and skills, not just on testing limits and being overinvolved with adults. It means that they have taken on powerful forces, from the media to loving relatives, that may want to force Cherub into chubby habits.

Having attained so many triumphs and formed so many kind habits, you are likely to find the next year much easier. With a few bumps, of course.

3

Toddlers: One to Three Years
LEARNING TO CHOOSE

Toddlers change shape quite a lot over the period between the ages of one to three years, from baby to little kid. As they do, weight gain is much slower. Helping a toddler grow into baby fat or to keep from acquiring too much of it is a huge investment in the future: In some ways, it's easier now than it will ever be again. This is because toddlers rely on parents, not peers, for their idea of what is normal. When it is normal to exercise vigorously, to eat planned snacks and meals without being coaxed or restricted, and to regard food as food (not as a bribe, reward, or punishment), it is much easier to keep weight gain in the appropriate range. Now and later, too.

TODDLER FAT FACTS

- Most toddlers gain about four and one-half pounds a year—that's only six ounces a month.
- Most toddlers need about 1,300 calories a day. For children under age two, 300 of those calories consist of their daily 16 ounces of whole milk.

- Many toddlers eat one good meal a day, and the rest of the time "just pick." What they eat can vary enormously from meal to meal, and from day to day. This is a normal pattern for many in the "just right" weight range.
- Statistically, little girls who gain too much weight in early childhood are likely to start this trend between the ages of one and two. This may be in part because they become very "girly" in their choice of activities and don't get much exercise.
- Statistically, little boys who gain too much weight in early childhood are likely to start this trend between the ages of two and three. This may be in part because they are in the power-mad, possessive stage of development, and food is a fine mode of expression. Or it may be because they are so energetic and exhausting that adults are driven to use food in order to get a moment's peace.

Damon's mom, Melissa, has brought her day-care charges to the office again! Six toddlers in a moderately small exam room, along for the ride so that Zea can have her ears checked. They are all amazingly well-behaved except for Camilla, who has perfected the art of sidling out the door; we realize she's missing (four times in this fifteen-minute visit) only when one of the medical assistants returns her from her adventures down the hallway.

Why it should occur to me to think of lining them up in some kind of order, I do not know. The task would clearly be impossible—like keeping six noodles of different lengths all twirled neatly around one fork.

But if I could, there would be a number of options. I could do it by age, with Camilla at fifteen months the youngest and Buster the oldest at nearly three years. Or by height, with Camilla the shortest and Scott the tallest. By sneakiness, with Camilla at the top and straightforward Damon at the bottom.

If I lined them up by chubbiness, there would be a group of four, and then a group of two. The first four would illustrate the normal progression from baby shape to preschool shape. There would be Camilla (if she could be found) with a chubby neck and a round belly that she likes to lift her shirt to show, with sturdy legs and filled-out arms. Then there's Damon, at twenty-one months, with a neck that looks neck-y and muscles showing through slightly padded arms and legs. His back curves in, and his cheerful tummy sticks out.

Jennifer, at thirty months, still has that back-curved, belly-sticking-out posture, but her arms and legs look longer and less padded than Damon's. And Scott, at thirty-four months, looks muscular, with just a slight back curve and a tummy that follows that curve, gently.

If you plotted these four on the Weight for Height curve, they would all be in the "just right" zone: somewhere between the 25th and 75th percentile curves.

Then, in a group by themselves, are Zea and Buster. Zea, at twenty months, waddles: Her thighs rub if she tries to walk with her feet straight. Her neck is obscured by an extra chin, and her belly doesn't just protrude; it jiggles. She doesn't climb and run with the agility of her age-mate Damon, or even of Camilla. She is as cute as a button.

And here is Buster, celebrating his third birthday next week. Buster is sturdy or stocky or stout. His deep voice goes with his hefty body. Next to him, nearly-three Scott looks thin—fragile, almost. Buster's belly has an aggressive air to it. It's not a belly that you feel like whuzzling; it's a belly intended for making its way in the world, pushing other people out of the path so that Buster can stride forward.

Both Zea and Buster are off the chart for weight for height.

Zea's Growth Charts

Like many little girls, Zea started gaining much of her weight at around her first birthday.

During her infancy, Zea grew at the 25th percentile for length. If you lined Zea up with 100 little girls the same age, she would be taller than 25 of them and shorter than 75 of them.

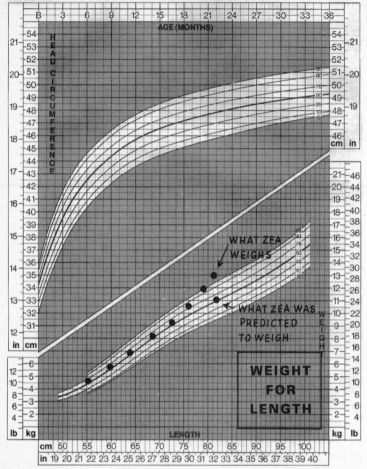

**GIRLS: BIRTH TO 36 MONTHS
PHYSICAL GROWTH
NCHS PERCENTILES** Name **ZEA** Record #___

WHAT ZEA WEIGHS

WHAT ZEA WAS PREDICTED TO WEIGH

WEIGHT FOR LENGTH

DATE	AGE	LENGTH	WEIGHT	HEAD CIRC.	COMMENT
	2 MOS.	21¾"	9¾ lbs.		
	4 MOS.	23½"	12 lbs.		
	6 MOS.	25¼"	14½ lbs.		
	9 MOS.	27"	18 lbs.		
	12 MOS.	28½"	21 lbs.		
	15 MOS.	30"	23 lbs.		
	18 MOS.	31¼"	26 lbs.		
	20 MOS.	32"	28 lbs.		

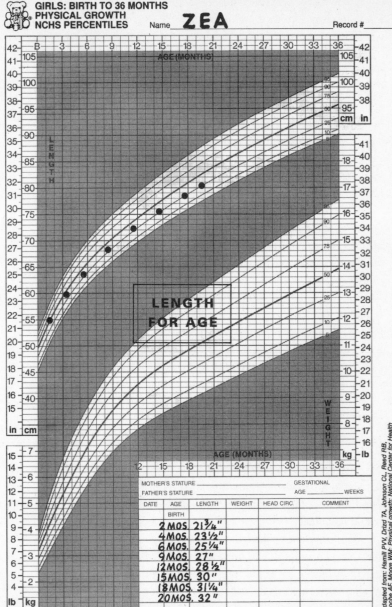

GIRLS: BIRTH TO 36 MONTHS
PHYSICAL GROWTH
NCHS PERCENTILES

Name **ZEA**

Record #

AGE (MONTHS)

LENGTH

cm in

LENGTH
FOR AGE

WEIGHT

AGE (MONTHS)

*Adapted from: Hamill PVV, Drizd TA, Johnson CL, Reed RB,
Roche AF, Moore WM: Physical growth: National Center for Health
Statistics percentiles. AM J CLIN NUTR 32:607-629, 1979. Data
from the Fels Longitudinal Study, Wright State University School of
Medicine, Yellow Springs, Ohio.

© 1982 Ross Products Division, Abbott Laboratories

MOTHER'S STATURE _____   GESTATIONAL
FATHER'S STATURE _____   AGE _____ WEEKS

DATE	AGE	LENGTH	WEIGHT	HEAD CIRC.	COMMENT
	BIRTH				
	2 MOS.	21¾"			
	4 MOS.	23½"			
	6 MOS.	25¼"			
	9 MOS.	27"			
	12 MOS.	28½"			
	15 MOS.	30"			
	18 MOS.	31¼"			
	20 MOS.	32"			

Her weight was average for her length, at the 50th percentile. If you lined up Zea with 100 little girls her length, 50 of them would weigh more and 50 of them would weigh less than Zea.

At her first birthday, Zea was twenty-eight and one-half inches long and weighed nearly twenty-one pounds.

At fifteen months, Zea had gained to twenty-three pounds. Her mother was concerned that she hadn't gained a pound a month, the way she had before she turned a year. But in fact Zea had gained more than was appropriate. On the Weight for Length chart, she had gone up to the 75th percentile. That is, if you lined up Zea with 100 little girls her height, 75 would weigh less than Zea and 25 would weigh more.

Between fifteen and eighteen months, Zea really did gain a pound a month. At eighteen months, Zea's weight for length was at the 95th percentile. If you lined up Zea with 100 little girls her height, 95 would weigh less than Zea and only 5 would weigh more.

At twenty months, today, Zea has continued to gain a pound a month, and she now weighs twenty-eight pounds. Her weight for length is now over the 95th percentile. If you lined up Zea with 100 little girls her length, all of them would weigh less than Zea. If Zea had continued on the curve that she had established as a baby, she would weigh only twenty-four pounds today.

Buster's Growth Charts

Like many little boys, Buster started gaining extra weight between the ages of two and three.

Buster has always been big. His length has been in the 90th percentile since birth. At any time, if you lined up Buster with 100 little boys the same age, 90 would be shorter, and only 10 would be taller.

On the Weight for Length chart, up to age two Buster was at the 75th percentile. If you lined up 100 little boys the same length as Buster, 75 would weigh less than Buster and 25 would weigh more. This was a "just right" weight for Buster.

At age two, Buster was thirty-six and one quarter inches long and weighed thirty-one pounds.

Over the next few months, Buster mastered Terrible Twoness. He whined and balked and demanded. Putting Buster in Time Out was no easy trick: He was big and energetic. Rewarding him for good behavior with sustained attention and happy voice and face was hard for both his tired parents, and for his day-care mother, Melissa. Rewarding with food seemed easier, and it actually worked—at least some of the time.

There were other factors. Meals and snacks became unavoidably erratic at home. It was hard for either parent to take Buster to the park on the weekends. Winter came, and going outside at day care meant galoshes and snowsuits. Usually the children would be out for five minutes, get cold, and have to come in for cookies and milk.

By thirty months of age, Buster weighed thirty-seven pounds. He'd gained a pound a month. On the Weight for Length chart, Buster was off the top of the chart, above the 95th percentile by one and one-half little boxes. If you lined up Buster with 100 little boys his height, all 100 would weigh less than Buster. The average little boy his length would weigh about thirty-three pounds.

At three, we plotted Buster on the bigger kids' version of charts: Boys 2 to 18. We measured him, standing up, at thirty-nine and one-half inches tall. He weighed forty-three pounds.

On the Weight for Height scale, he is now two little boxes above the top percentile, the 95th. If 100 little boys of the same height as Buster lined up with him in order of weight, Buster wouldn't only be at the top of the line; he'd be standing some distance away from the next little boy.

If Buster continues to gain a pound a month, by the time he is four he will weigh fifty-two pounds. If he continues—as expected—to grow along the 90th percentile for height, he will be forty-two and one-half inches tall at that point. According to the numbers on the Weight for Height chart, Buster will then be five little boxes above the top line on the chart. The average little boy that height—the one at the 50th percentile—weighs just under forty pounds. If Buster had stayed on his original 75th percentile, he would be weighing just under forty-two pounds. He is ten pounds over his "just right" range.

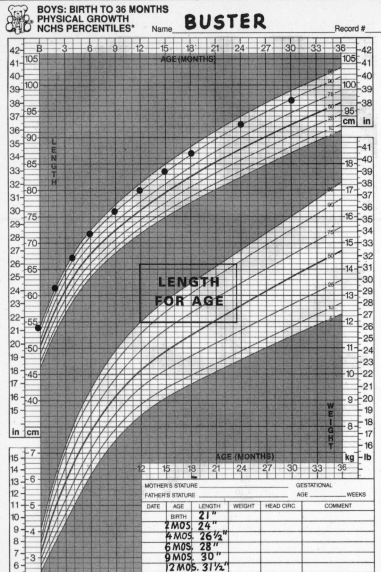

**BOYS: BIRTH TO 36 MONTHS
PHYSICAL GROWTH
NCHS PERCENTILES***

Name **BUSTER**

Record #_____

AGE (MONTHS)

LENGTH

LENGTH FOR AGE

AGE (MONTHS)

WEIGHT

MOTHER'S STATURE _____
FATHER'S STATURE _____

GESTATIONAL
AGE _____ WEEKS

DATE	AGE	LENGTH	WEIGHT	HEAD CIRC	COMMENT
	BIRTH	21"			
	2 MOS.	24"			
	4 MOS.	26½"			
	6 MOS.	28"			
	9 MOS.	30"			
	12 MOS.	31½"			
	15 MOS.	33"			
	18 MOS.	34½"			
	24 MOS.	36¼"			
	30 MOS.	38¼"			

*Adapted from: Hamill PVV, Drizd TA, Johnson CL, Reed RB, Roche AF, Moore WM: Physical growth: National Center for Health Statistics percentiles. AM J CLIN NUTR 32:607-629, 1979. Data from the Fels Longitudinal Study, Wright State University School of Medicine, Yellow Springs, Ohio.

© 1982 Ross Products Division, Abbott Laboratories

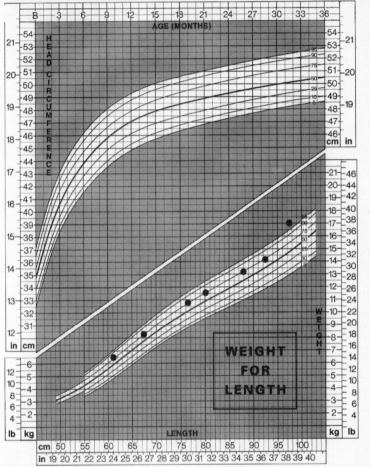

BOYS: BIRTH TO 36 MONTHS
PHYSICAL GROWTH
NCHS PERCENTILES*

Name **BUSTER**   Record #

DATE	AGE	LENGTH	WEIGHT	HEAD CIRC.	COMMENT
	2 MOS.	24"	14 lbs.		
	4 MOS.	26½"	18 lbs.		
	9 MOS.	30"	23½ lbs.		
	12 MOS.	31½"	25¼ lbs.		
	18 MOS.	34½"	29 lbs.		
	24 MOS.	36¼"	31 lbs.		
	30 MOS.	38¼"	37 lbs.		

Name **BUSTER**   Record #

	MOTHER'S STATURE		FATHER'S STATURE	
DATE	AGE	STATURE	WEIGHT	COMMENT
TODAY	3 YRS.	39½"	43 lbs.	
NEXT YEAR	4 YRS.	42½"		

AGE (YEARS)

STATURE

HEIGHT FOR AGE

WEIGHT

AGE (YEARS)

*Adapted from: Hamill PVV, Drizd TA, Johnson CL, Reed RB,
Roche AF, Moore WM: Physical growth: National Center for Health
Statistics percentiles. AM J CLIN NUTR 32:607-629, 1979. Data
from the National Center for Health Statistics (NCHS), Hyattsville,
Maryland.

© 1982 Ross Products Division, Abbott Laboratories

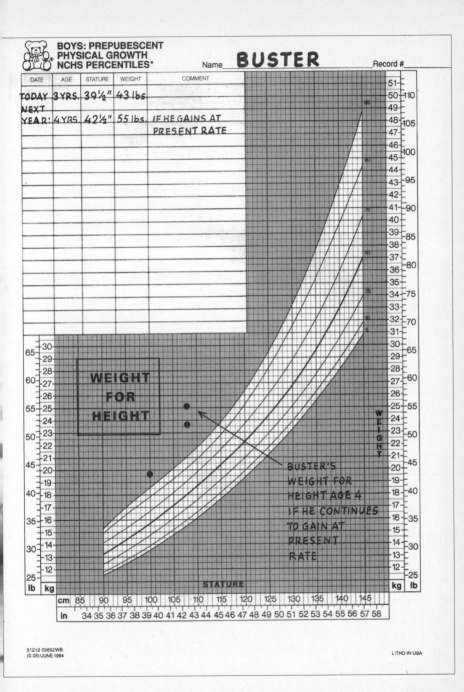

BOYS: PREPUBESCENT PHYSICAL GROWTH NCHS PERCENTILES*

Name **BUSTER**

Record #

DATE	AGE	STATURE	WEIGHT	COMMENT
TODAY	3 YRS.	39½"	43 lbs	
NEXT YEAR:	4 YRS.	42½"	55 lbs.	IF HE GAINS AT PRESENT RATE

WEIGHT FOR HEIGHT

BUSTER'S WEIGHT FOR HEIGHT AGE 4 IF HE CONTINUES TO GAIN AT PRESENT RATE

STATURE

51212 09892WB
(0.05)/JUNE 1994

LITHO IN USA

THE GOAL

The goals from the ages of one to three are: allowing the natural slowdown in weight gain and appetite, allowing the change in shape from adorable infant to cute little kid, and designing an environment in which it is easy to use up the day's calories by growing and being active.

No toddler, no matter how chubby, should lose weight during this period. The brain still grows rapidly until age two and for a time thereafter. It is not worth taking any chance of depriving the brain of calories. The goal for the Zeas and Busters is to slow down their rate of weight gain, perhaps to two or three pounds a year, as they grow into their height. We'll look at this in detail later.

THE CHALLENGE

It's not hard for a toddler to gain extra weight during this time. There are lots of reasons why.

A toddler's weight gain is *supposed to slow down dramatically* at about a year of age. Thus, a toddler's growth in appetite is *supposed to diminish dramatically* at about a year of age. Because they don't realize that this is normal, many parents are thrown into a state of shock by the event and worry that their child is wasting away. They double up on snacks and tempt Cherub with high-calorie treats.

This is particularly easy to do because Cherub has a new relationship with food these days.

It's the peak age for imitation. If you nibble a few chips and dip while watching "Sesame Street" with toddlers, they must have a bag for themselves. If you sip a glass of Diet Coke while fixing dinner, Cherub must have a cup of apple juice while she "helps."

Then there's finicky eating, which results in coaxing to eat.

Toddlers are like adolescents. There's a need to be a baby, as well as a need to be In Charge. This leads to lots of expressions of ambivalence. One of them is finicky eating—proving a point by refusing a previously loved food, or refusing to try something new, or whatever.

Loving parents, worried that Cherub "isn't eating a thing" or "isn't taking enough fluid," rush in with spoonfuls laden with food and ploys about Here Comes the Choo Choo Train into the Station. Or with juice to make the water taste better. And Cherub, ambivalent about independence and pleased to be the center of attention, is very likely to eat beyond what nature suggests.

Toddlers may also spend a fair amount of time waiting: carpooling to day care, running errands with the day-care group, sitting in waiting rooms, standing in line. With waiting, there is boredom. A toddler is a force of nature to be reckoned with. Food is a mighty force in the arsenal of the adult leader. It can quell rebellion, soothe hurt feelings, and distract the aggressive or the bored. It makes waiting worthwhile and wandering off less attractive.

Also, it can be difficult to be sure that toddlers are really getting as much exercise as you think they are.

Any groups containing toddlers are a cross between a three-ring circus and a militant uprising. There is noise, chaos, and frequent discontent; aggression, tantrums, and wandering off. Toddlers need a lot of supervision, and because no adult can be everywhere at one time, most day-care centers are designed for safety and easy supervision. There may not be a lot of room to run and climb, and there may also not be much encouragement to do so.

This is the age when addiction to television begins. A toddler or group of toddlers who would otherwise be in perpetual motion, otherwise known as exercise, can be stopped in midtumble by a video or a TV program.

Starting at about eighteen months, children and parents become very gender-aware. Little girls may prefer—and parents may encourage them to prefer—sedentary play with dolls and crayons and puzzles. Little boys may prefer—and parents may encourage them to prefer—pretend games with weapons. At this age, as opposed to later on, such play may involve a great deal of shouting and waving of swords but not much running around. Toddlers this age just don't have the coordination to wave a sword and dash about at the same time. Starting at age two, there comes to be an enormous range of energy expended and calories burned. Even in the same family, even in the same day-care center.

Zea and Buster may have been born with a slightly greater delight in oral activities; or a slightly more efficient metabolism for turning calories into fat; or a slightly higher interest in sedentary versus physical activities. But what has tipped the scale, in both senses of the phrase, is only this: They have grown up in an environment in which it was very easy and very tempting to eat a few more calories than they burned, nearly every day, for a long time.

THE ASSESSMENT

At around the first birthday, toddlers enter a new growth phase, one that seems startlingly different from the one that was evident the past year. During the first six months of life, babies gained an ounce a day—about two pounds a month. During the second six months, they gained half an ounce a day—about a pound a month.

Now they will gain only about three to five pounds in a whole year—about four to seven *ounces* a month.

No wonder that parents are often concerned at the fifteen-month visit. "But she's only gained a pound! Doesn't she look skinny?" At fifteen months, double chins and deep creases in the upper arms and thighs have just about disappeared. You still shouldn't see ribs or vertebrae showing, and there's still a lovely big belly sticking out, though. By two, that belly still sticks out, but in a compact kind of curve that is nearly parallel to the natural curve of the spine. By three, that belly is beginning to vanish.

With Zea and Buster, it's easy to tell that they weigh too much. But sometimes it's not so evident. A Nearly-Three who is on the too plump side may not look fat; he or she may just look like an oversized one-year-old with a protruding belly and chubby arms

and legs. A toddler who is over the 90th percentile of weight for height is very probably carrying too much of that weight as fat.

Happily, toddlers who are already weighing more than the top of of their "just right" range have lots of months and years in which to slow down their weight gain as they grow in height. Parents of toddlers can control what is offered to them to eat and how many enticing opportunities they have for exercise. This is perhaps the easiest time to help a child grow into extra baby fat.

THE PLAN

Any plan to help the Zeas and the Busters must deal with the toddler mentality. We know from lots of research that toddlers are able to judge how much they should eat; that is, they can adjust to a previous big or little meal, and to whether they've been very active or not. To do this, they need a few helps. First, they need nutritious food given on a regular schedule—not as constant handouts to stave off whining or acting up. Second, they need respect for their ability to choose how much of what they eat. No coaxing, nagging, punishment. And no effusive praise and clapping, either. Just company and conversation.

Along the same lines, you can't force a toddler to exercise. You need to create an enticing situation.

Exercise and Activity

The activity level at this age is at least as important as diet in determining whether or not a toddler will grow chubby or continue to be chubby during this period.

Exercise is under the control of the person who spends the daytime hours with the toddler. If those hours are mostly spent waiting, marking time, watching TV, taking naps, or otherwise in inactivity, then the toddler is at risk not just for chubbiness but also for emotional, intellectual, and social immaturity ahead.

Toddlers need lots of room and safe challenges for their activities. Ones need to throw and roll balls and push around wheeled toys; they need to climb and to practice running. Twos need places in which to run, slides and swings, wheeled toys to pedal, balls to throw or even hit. Ones and Twos both need trucks and cars to push around, places to explore, and hand skills to practice.

They need someone to design this environment, teach them how to use it, enforce reasonable and consistent limits without spanking or screaming or making them feel terrible. They need someone, that is, with an enormous amount of energy and with no other tasks or diversions—like errands or housework or talking on the phone or watching TV—to absorb them.

Toddlers who are watchers of the world, who like to sit and assess and look at books and play with dollies, need an adult to lure them into activity and social engagement. Toddlers who have watched a lot of TV and want to stand around fascinated by toy swords or guns, making loud, threatening noises, need an adult to lure them into activity and social engagement, too.

Active toddlers are at an enormous advantage in avoiding increasing chubbiness. The reason is that it is not binge eating that makes a child grow inexorably fat. It is a matter of a relatively small number of extra calories a day—calories that aren't burned off in growth and exercise. That number of extra calories can be quite small. Fifty unburned calories a day for a year will yield five pounds of extra fat. Five pounds extra is a lot at this age. It would mean gaining nine pounds a year instead of the expected four pounds.

It's easy to eat an extra fifty calories a day over what you usually eat. Three extra ounces of apple juice. Two graham crackers. Half a cup of Cheerios, one at a time over five or six hours.

If you're active and running around, you'll burn those off. But if you are sitting around—in the car, in front of the TV, in a waiting room—you won't.

So in concentrating on creating an environment in which it's easy not to get chubby, the first thing to look at is not the kitchen but at the play yard and play room, the attitude and energy of the caregiver, and the ambience of the whole place. If there are no playmates, if all the other children are infants or much older, that's a problem. If there are lots of forbidden temptations as a toddler tries to explore and climb, that's a problem.

Moreover, starting at the age of two, toddlers begin to demonstrate extremely different interests and temperaments.

For instance, most can run, climb, throw, kick a ball. Some can jump. A few can pedal a tricycle. But some of them choose to do so; others do not. Some are encouraged to do so; others are actively prevented—by environment or by caregivers that can't tolerate so much activity.

Girlness and Boyness are important concepts now, for toddlers and for parents; and girls may choose or be led into quieter pursuits than boys.

Finally, older children have an influence on Twos. Some Twos will be included in their older siblings' or day-care mates' games and will want to do everything those Gods do; others will be excluded and perhaps relegated to a part of the house where running around isn't possible or allowed.

Finally, some Twos are already watching a great deal of TV. Many spend two hours or more, often watching the same beloved video, every single day.

A loving adult who can analyze a toddler's lifestyle along all these lines and gently intervene can make a world of difference.

Nutrition

The slowdown in growth means a shift in appetite. Most toddlers, starting at a year of age, eat a good breakfast, a fair lunch, and not much dinner.

When your child spends the daytime out of your sight, this pattern can be very discombobulating.

Breakfast is often rushed. You may not be able to remember what *you* ate, much less what anybody else ate. You don't see your toddler for lunch. And then comes dinnertime, and "he just picks at his food."

You see the baby fat melting away. You may very well worry. Even if you don't worry, it can be a bit, well, poignant. Even I, who have known, say, Millie, from birth feel a pang at that eighteen-month-old visit. Suddenly Millie is not a baby any more.

Keep bearing in mind that this change is normal. And that it goes along with that big task of the toddler: developing independence and autonomy—being in charge of setting his or her own goals and achieving them. Many of these goals will involve accepting or rejecting food.

By a year of age, most babies do a pretty good job feeding themselves with fingers and bottle; a large number can hold their own cups.

By fifteen months, they all can hold their cups, and many have interesting ways of using the spoon. Some scoop, reverse position, and get into the mouth whatever has stuck in the bowl of the upside-down spoon. Others still get a fair amount of food into other facial orifices. Many use their fingers to fill the bowl of the spoon. There's a lot of banging, flinging, and using the spoon as a catapult.

By eighteen months, most have learned to use a spoon, and sometimes even a fork, neatly, spilling little.

Self-feeding can be a joy and a source of endless comical home videos, or it can be a battle. If it's a battle, it's unwinnable by either toddler or loving adult. Toddlers who "win" and eat only the foods they find perfectly appealing may become too fat or even malnourished, missing out on necessary nutrients. If the loving adult "wins," this means only that toddler has been distracted into eating as an occupation having nothing to do with hunger and everything to do with power, deception, and manipulation.

There are three big rules of toddler eating.

RULE 1: The adult decides what variety of foods to offer.

COROLLARY: If toddler is really going to be making choices, all the options need to be equally acceptable. So don't offer an "airlines meal" with entree, veggie, roll, and dessert all equal choices, and then get upset because the toddler eats only the roll and the dessert.

RULE 2: The toddler decides how much of each to eat.

COROLLARY: This happens without anybody bribing, luring, rewarding, begging, pleading, cajoling; without anybody criticizing, acting hurt, getting angry, or using the leftover food as a threat or punishment.

RULE 3: Adults decide the maximum, but not the minimum, offered of any given food or drink.

COROLLARY: There is an art to this. See below.

Milk

During the year from one to two, whole milk is recommended. Ones need the essential fatty acids in whole milk for their continuing rapid brain development.

When toddler turns two it makes a lot of sense to change to 1% or even to nonfat milk, or to mix the two. Whole milk has just too much fat and lowfat milk doesn't cut the number of fat calories enough to make a difference.

Food

Calorie needs can vary during this age range, but not by huge amounts. Many Ones grow appropriately on 1,000 calories a day; many Twos, on 1,200. A few very tall or extremely active Ones may need 1,200 calories a day; a few Twos may need 1,400 calories.

Calories spent on snacks and "munchy" handouts can tip the balance from "just right" daily menus to chub-inducing ones. Moreover, the munchy foods are usually very poor in nutrition: Either they don't contain much except fat or sugar, or what they do contain is redundant—the toddler is getting plenty in regular meals. A more appropriate use of these "extra" calories might be to "use" them for the occasional real dessert or treat or birthday cake.

MEALS

Here's a menu of what might be offered to a toddler from One to Three. Notice the size of the servings.

Breakfast might consist of two ounces of orange juice (28 calories), half a cup of Rice Krispies (56 calories), half a banana (50 calories), and a slice of sourdough toast with butter (80 calories). That's 214 calories.

Lunch could be one-half sandwich made with one slice of sourdough and one slice of bologna with a little mustard, 1 ounce of cheese spread, and no butter (89 for bologna, 72 for bread, 82 for cheese; that's 243 calories); half a cup of applesauce (97 calories): total, 340 calories.

Dinner might be half a cup of macaroni and cheese (256 calories), a half cup of cooked peas without butter (67 calories), and half a canned pear in syrup (58 calories). That's 381 calories.

WHAT HELPS

- Check out how much exercise your toddler really gets. Don't assume that he or she "runs around all day at day care."
- Make each meal include something delicious from the toddler's point of view.
- Give appropriate-sized servings. For Twos, this means three or four portions of about half a cup each, not any bigger than a playing card from a regular deck.
- When you read labels, make sure that you evaluate the serving size. It's all very well to read that one serving of cold cuts contains only sixty calories, with thirty-six of them fat; it's quite another to learn that this "serving" is only one lone slice that really looks more like a tidbit. Or that one single slice of processed cheese contains seventy calories, with forty-five of them fat. Or that one "serving" of peanut butter or mayonnaise as described on the label is only one tablespoon.
- Postpone catsup and mayonnaise for as long as you can.
- Let dessert be a fruit most days. When dessert is fancier, don't make a big deal about it or use it as a bribe or reward. Not only does that make the dessert too important, but it also devalues the rest of the meal.

Snacks might be three ounces of iron-fortified apple juice and two animal crackers, and at another time, most of a small banana.

That's a total of about 150 calories.

Milk should be 16 ounces a day of whole milk for Ones (300 calories). Sixteen ounces a day of nonfat or 1% milk for Twos (180 to 200 calories).

This is a nice, varied menu. Most toddlers will like it. It comes to about 1,382 calories with whole milk and 1,282 or so with nonfat milk.

Most Ones need only about 1,000 calories a day. So don't be surprised if One can't finish the whole day's menu. A Two, on the other hand, might finish every bite.

This menu gives plenty of calcium and iron, a variety of foods, and some fiber. It's not a holier-than-thou menu; there's apple juice and animal crackers for a little fun.

FATS

Until age two, babies get carte blanche when it comes to fats. They need essential fatty acids for brain growth. More than 40 percent of their daily calories may be eaten as fats.

After age two, though, there's no need for a diet in which 40 percent or more of the calories come from fat, and there are some good reasons to monitor fat a bit. The current recommendation of the American Academy of Pediatrics and the American Heart Association is to aim for a diet in which 30 percent of the calories come from fat.

For Twos who are over their "just right" range of weight, this makes special good sense. Not only are we helping them to grow into their present weight; we are hoping to form food tastes that will stand them in good stead for the future.

But nobody wants to have to count fat calories.

I will ask your indulgence, however, for just a moment as we look at the sample menu given previously. It contains about 1,382 calories. Thirty percent of these should be fat—that is, about 414 calories.

However, most Twos need only 1,200 calories a day. They won't eat all of that daily menu. So 360 calories as fat (30 percent of 1,200) would be a better goal.

If Two drinks whole milk, the total number of calories in this daily menu is 448 fat calories.

That's more than recommended—not by a little, but by rather a lot.

However, if Two drinks 1% milk, this brings the amount of fat down 108 calories, to about 340 calories.

So the first thing to remember is that the easiest way to reduce fat calories for Twos and older is to reduce the fat in the milk.

Going to low-fat 2% milk doesn't usually do the trick; it's too close to whole milk in fat content (42 calories of fat in 8 ounces rather than 64 calories).

Now, look at the menu again. There aren't any fried foods or gooey desserts. Butter isn't added to the sandwich or to the peas. If Two is getting daily menus that feature these delicacies routinely, then I don't know how we're going to get the total calories and the fat calories into the range we want.

A lesson in life.

FAST FOOD

There's the fast food you get at a food chain, and the fast food you pick up from the deli or frozen-foods section of the grocery store.

As an occasional treat, that's fine. But if it's a regular part of a toddler's diet, I'd be careful.

For instance, the lunch described in the menu above has 340 calories with 135 fat calories, just a bit over that magic 30 percent mark.

Compare this with a couple of fast food alternatives. Here is a delectable-looking little packet of tidy foods, the Lunchables by Oscar Mayer. Everything in it is a nice toddler shape: rectangular cheese, round crackers, round bologna, all looking toddler sized.

Total calories: 480. Total fat calories: 330.

And here is a Quarter-Pounder with Cheese from McDonald's. The sandwich in its entirety?

Total calories: 525. Total fat calories: 284.

If a meal has more than half of its calories as fat, it may be hard to bring the total daily menu into line so that it contains 30 percent of its calories as fat.

This may not matter so much to a toddler who is average or below in weight for height, but it can make a big difference to our Zeas and Busters.

BELOVED FOODS

Barbecued spare ribs. Enchiladas. Ding Dongs. Fried chicken, cole slaw, french fries. Sweet-and-sour pork. Any kind of pie. Hot fudge sundaes.

It is too painful to contemplate the total and fat calorie fallout of these wonderful dishes. Most of us know instinctively that they are way over the recommended amount.

Toddlers are human, too. They tend to love these dishes, and when toddlers love something they make no secret of it. It is very gratifying to see one's food offering get such a response.

Again, the toddler who is thin or average in the Weight for Height range could have these foods fairly often. They are moderately nutritious. If the rest of the diet tries for reasonableness, there's no problem.

But for Zea and Buster, who already clearly love to eat, these dishes can be trouble. Zea and Buster have been known to eat adult-sized portions of any one of the foregoing items.

Should you serve them just once in a while, as a treat? Yes. Should you serve them to the rest of the family, but make toddler a different meal? Not a chance. Toddlers have superb olfactory devices and can detect the presence of something delicious from rooms and even houses away.

JUICE AS A BEVERAGE INSTEAD OF WATER

Juice as a beverage is highly overrated.

By "as a beverage," I mean carrying around those little boxes or bottles of juice, or putting juice rather than water into a workout bottle, or diluting water with juice so that the water "has some taste."

What is so upsetting is that parents and other loving adults feel that giving juice is a caring, responsible way of providing a healthful, wholesome beverage that is good for the child: that the juice contains vitamins and minerals. After all, the ads stress "wholesomeness" and "purity" and "goodness of the fruit itself."

Here are the juices that have no, or truly insignificant, amounts, of vitamin C, vitamin A, B vitamins, calcium, and iron. Unless they are fortified artificially, these juices contain nothing except sugar and potassium. Potassium is contained in so many other foods, it's hard to be deficient in it unless there is a medical problem.

Apple juice
Bottled grape juice (frozen has some Vitamin C)
Papaya nectar
Peach nectar
Pear nectar
Pineapple juice
Prune juice

Many children I see who drink these juices, as a single juice or as a mix, drink them literally as if they were water.

Of course, the problem here isn't merely one of empty calories. Children who drink juice all the time will often refuse both water and milk—and who can blame them?

Not only do they miss out on the nutrition of milk, but they don't gain an appreciation of water as the thing you drink when you are thirsty. So guess what happens during the teenage and adult years: Sodaville. Or Boozeville.

Also, as you may have noticed yourself, sugar and salt make you thirsty. I know of no study to buttress my suspicion, but I do have a sneaky idea that the sugar (and the salts in some juices) provokes thirst so that the drinker seeks out *more* juice, which provokes more thirst so that the drinker . . . you see what I mean.

Now, some juices are fortified with iron, vitamin C, calcium, and perhaps other good stuff that I haven't run into. The only way to tell is to read the label. Of course, if your preschooler is getting iron from meats, fish, chicken, and green leafy vegetables; calcium from dairy products; and vitamin C from raw tomatoes or other veggies (see the Appendix) or naturally rich citrus fruits or juices like orange and grapefruit juice, you may ask: Why give juice that is artificially fortified?

I don't know. I don't even know what that "natural goodness" is that those juices listed above are supposed to contain. If you find out, please let me know.

Three ounces of orange or grapefruit juice with breakfast will give a preschooler the entire daily requirement of vitamin C. So will three ounces of Cranberrry Cocktail. (Cranberry *juice* is so bitter as to be undrinkable.) You do need a fresh daily infusion of vitamin C, and this amount of this kind of juice is a nice way to get it.

Six ounces of apple juice amounts to ninety calories. Most of the children who consume apple juice as an all-day beverage drink three or four times that amount every day.

Some noncitrus juices do have nutritional benefits. Grape juice that is frozen, not bottled, contains about half the amount of vitamin C as orange juice.

Apricot nectar contains a fair amount of vitamin A: one ounce gives about 10 percent of the daily recommended amount. Of course, vitamin A is well represented in all yellow veggies and fruits, so it's hard to think of somebody desperately needing that 10 percent

Apricot nectar and prune juice are both good for constipation.

I've never seen a child drinking prune juice as a beverage preferred to water.

SNACKS

Of course toddlers can have snacks. A well-designed snack is a great pick-me-up, and a bit of respite for the caregiver.

Continuous handouts to eat and drink, like juice and crackers and raisins, aren't snacks. Continuous handouts pose major problems for all toddlers, not just for those whose weight gain is too rapid. First, they befuddle the internal regulators that tell the toddler when and how much to eat. Second, they provide a continuous mouth environment of acid and sugar and can lead to cavities in the baby teeth.

In the menu given previously, the snacks fit into the total daily calorie and fat calorie count. Yes, even though one of the snacks was apple juice and animal crackers. There is practically no fat in either snack, and the total number of calories is only about 150—a bit over 10 percent of the total daily calories.

This is a good guide for snacks. It gives you much more flexibility in your meal menus.

Another option: Serve a portion of the last or next meal as a snack. See the Appendix for more snack suggestions.

SPREADS AND TOPPINGS

Have you ever known someone who would eat anything (I mean anything) if there were catsup or mayonnaise on it?

That's one good reason not to start this habit now. Catsup has only fifteen calories in one tablespoon; the problem is, people don't eat just one tablespoon. Toddlers who really like catsup or are really "addicted" to it may be consuming a couple of ounces a day, just about every day. Hard to stop (but worth it). Easy to prevent.

At least catsup has no fat. Mayonnaise has ninety-nine calories in a tablespoon, and they are all fat.

Measure out a tablespoon of either catsup and mayonnaise, just to get an idea of what you're dealing with. See how small an amount it is spread on bread or other foods.

Redefining the "Good Eater"

In toddler terms, a good eater isn't one who cleans his or her plate, or one who always tries something new without fuss, and usually likes it. Such toddlers do exist, but they are rare; and some of them are so "good" about eating that they eat more than they need. Toddler Good Eaters are those who select appropriate amounts of the foods presented to them, eat them with enjoyment, and then stop and go on to other activities. The trick is to recognize this style as the very best one and not to try to change it.

But many toddlers fulfill neither definition of the Good Eater. These are the finicky ones, and there are several styles to choose from.

FINICKY EATERS

Most common is the Situational Refuser. After their first birthdays, and often long before, most toddlers regard the approach of a loaded spoon with something approaching a Red Alert:

Me do it self! If you insist on feeding me, I will dig in my heels and shut my mouth tight even while I howl and in general drive you bonkers.

This is particularly likely to happen if you are trying to feed Cherub in a hurry, or in the presence of company.

Next most common are the Performers.

I prefer to play rather than eat,

goes the unwritten, unspoken script of the Performer.

Left to my own devices, I will clearly starve. In order for me to survive, you must prepare meals to lure me. Make just my favorite foods, please, and you will have to guess which ones those are today because they certainly aren't the ones I made you prepare every day for the last three weeks. Then you will have to pursue me around the house, because I won't sit still in the high chair or at my little table. Or maybe I will, but I will bring my trains, the book about frogs, and my tiny dolly. You will have to pretend to give the dolly and Ben the Train a spoonful each time before I will consent to open my mouth.

Then there's the Pseudo-Gourmet. This one comes in several guises. There's the one who refuses to eat (usually) vegetables and most fruits and prefers (usually) starches—bread, pasta, rice, bananas—and maybe some meats, preferably bologna and hot dogs. Then there's the dairy fan, who refuses everything but milk and cheese, with a little yogurt for variety. And the milk refuser, who will drink only juice (often juice that is "watered down").

Whatever the profile of a particular Finicky Eater, the same question arises:

How can somebody so finicky become plump? Somebody who "eats like a bird" and refuses even to taste heavenly dishes? Somebody who has to be coaxed to try even one tiny crumb of lasagna?

Ask your own pediatrician, but in over two decades of practice I have never seen any toddlers waste away because their demands weren't catered to. I have, however, seen many a beleaguered parent, grandparent, and nanny held in thrall by the tiny and very well-nourished dictator. And I have seen many a chubby finicky eater.

It's easy to be finicky and chubby. All you need to do is to prefer a high-fat, high-calorie diet, and then get your loving adults all worked up about the fact that you're not eating enough.

WHAT TO DO?

As noted earlier, the only solution for the Situational Refuser is to avoid getting into high pressure situations in the first place. Remember, you cannot make a child eat.

Dealing with a Performer requires more self-discipline and histrionic skills. You must pretend that you do not care whether, or what, the performer deigns to consume. No more chasing around the house. No more feeding dollies and trains and imaginary playmates.

The trick is to set up a normal, pleasant meal situation and to radiate the calm expectation that the Performer will participate. It helps to involve even the youngest toddler in helping with the meal. Even a One can be a "taster." An older toddler can help stir something that isn't hot or that doesn't splash too much. A still older one can put napkins and spoons on a table.

Then you put the food on the plate and the toddler in the high chair (even if he or she is objecting) or the little chair or whatever. Then you put your plate on the table and sit down and start to eat, while talking with the toddler pleasantly, but not pleadingly, and not about the food. Eat your own food as if it tastes good but without a lot of "yum yum yums." Older toddlers, in particular, will realize that you are trying to goad them into eating and will dig in their heels. If you want to read a story aloud while the meal goes on, that sometimes helps to defuse any tension that might be left over from the old disgarded games of chase-and-feed.

Performers may escape from chair or high chair without eating a thing. If they do, pleasantly remove the plate, saying "I guess you're all done with lunch." If they then come back pleading, you could give them one more try—but don't get your hopes up. If they then do not eat, then the plate is gone for good. If they *do* eat, don't react as if they've achieved some amazing feat; merely smile and say you are glad they enjoyed their lunch. Then down from the table and on to something else.

If the toddler eats nothing or hardly anything, serve a small planned snack about two hours later. If the toddler whines and asks for the snack sooner than that, say that it isn't snacktime yet. For snack, serve a smaller, very pretty plate of the food he or she didn't eat for lunch. Don't comment on this, or on whether or not he or she eats any snack.

Continue to give a meal or a snack every two hours, maintaining the same cheerful, calm, and slightly preoccupied demeanor. Try to have the hours between be interesting and cheerful and active.

Don't let Performer fill up on juice or milk. Give the same servings of milk you always do (about sixteen ounces a day; see the following section on nutrition) and only the small juice serving for breakfast that gives toddler his or her daily vitamin C.

If you show by your behavior that Performers will not lose face by breaking down and feeding themselves—that you won't feel that you've won—you will see an almost immediate cure of the mealtime battle. Remember, toddlers who are drinking sixteen ounces of milk a day won't starve; and three or four missed meals (it's almost never that many) won't do them any harm at all.

When Performers do eat, don't insist on spoon over fingers; just have the spoon there and let them decide when they're going to use it.

If you try all this but find the pattern impossible to break, do talk with your pediatrician. Sometimes such power struggles need a little extra intervention. Food is enormously symbolic stuff, and feeding one's own child may bring back memories rife with emotion.

Chubbiness is not the only, or even the main, thing at stake here.

Tackling the Pseudo-Gourmet is usually much easier. For one thing, the emotions are easier. Usually the loving adult isn't scared or worried but rather feels resentful and more than a little bit manipulated. These are quite appropriate emotions.

When One gets on a food jag, there is only a single way to approach the situation: with good humor and lightheartedness and a calm determination not to go out of your way to accommodate it.

For instance, here is One with a plate before her. On that plate sit four portions, each about half the size of a playing card. These are of meatloaf, macaroni and cheese, green peas, and fruit cocktail. She has been demanding macaroni and cheese *only,* two meals a day, for the last ten days. You have stocked up on the gooey, bland mess, but you're not very comfortable with the situation.

One scarfs down the macaroni and cheese and makes her noise for more.

The universal urge is to say, "No more until you finish what's left on your plate!"

Alas, this leads to screams and retchings and battles and tears all round. Eventually, somebody gives in. Maybe toddler throws the whole plate on the floor and leaves, hungry and pathetic.

Or toddler eats everything on the plate (or everything she doesn't cleverly sneak elsewhere: neck crevice, overall pocket, the dog, the floor). By that time, she's clearly full but demands more macaroni and cheese, which she devours. Then she either throws up or spends an hour lying around like a lump, whining.

Or loving adult gives in—perhaps after saving face by making toddler take "just one bite" of all the other foods—and makes another two or more portions of macaroni and cheese.

This isn't fun even the first time, and it becomes quite wearing.

THE SOLUTION

The solution is to say, "That's all the macaroni and cheese there is for lunch (or dinner)." Stop there. Say no more. Remember Disraeli: "Never apologize; never explain." If it worked for the British empire, it will work for you.

If Finicky Eater refuses to eat a bite of anything else, remember: *It's not your fault!* Your duty was to present a plate of delicious, nutritious food. You did. *Her* job is to eat it. Merely say, "Lunch is over if you have finished eating. Now let's get those balls to play with!"

Two hours later, when Finicky Eater wants a snack, don't give her juice or crackers or cookies. If the meal she refused at lunch contained scrumptious, delicious morsels, offer her that—but dressed up: as a tiny mini-meal on its own, new plate, with a garnish. But never use that leftover meal as a punishment, or as a threat: "If you don't eat it now, you'll get it for dinner." If the leftovers don't look appealing to you, they won't look appealing to her, either. Instead, serve a healthy snack: cheese or fruit with a bit of her daily allowance of milk. Each meal is a new chance.

If Finicky Eater *does* eat everything—or even something else, just one thing—on the plate, don't go overboard with joy. It's always nice to say, "I'm glad you liked the meatloaf. My daddy taught me how to make it when I was a little boy." But don't reward her with a cookie, or go quick and call Mommy or Grandma and rejoice over the phone while Finicky Eater listens to every word, or do a celebration dance on the dining room table.

There is a variant on the Pseudo-Gourmet: The Addicted Pseudo-Gourmet. This young person wants, every day, for every meal, something that is not very good for him or her but that has addictive qualities. Usually, it is something salty or fatty. The big contenders are cold cuts and hot dogs, though sometimes it will be peanut butter. (This is a double problem because peanut butter can be dangerous. Toddlers can choke on peanut butter, especially if they eat it in globs; and the Heimlich maneuver is not likely to work.)

Addicted Pseudo-Gourmets can be very hard to deal with. Theirs is not a preference based entirely on power issues but on the enticing oral adventure of eating one particular food. There will be tears and tantrums, frantic searchings in the pantry and pullings upon the refrigerator handle.

If you are having problems standing your ground with the Addicted Pseudo-Gourmet, bear in mind that there are likely to be problems later on if you don't intervene now. When you remain addicted into kindergarten, you will learn to trade your healthy lunch of water-packed tuna and fruit for someone else's salami and cheese and Ding Dong.

Toddlerhood is about power and ownership, if it's about anything. Toddlers need power and ownership over their appetites and their choices of food—not over *you*.

THE MORAL OF THE STORY

The goal of these two years is not just to help toddlers maintain, or attain, "just right" weight. It's to take the first step in a lifelong pattern of healthy eating and exercise.

How toddlers feel about themselves, the people in authority over them, and their abilities to conquer their worlds set the stage for success later on. Toddlers who feel adorable, clever, and capable and who trust that limits will be set consistently, reasonably, and firmly have a huge advantage as they toddle into the preschool years.

Toddlers who have meals and snacks set out at regular times and who are allowed to choose freely what and how much of what is offered have a big head start in being able to eat wisely. Avoiding highly "addicting" foods does toddlers a big favor in this regard.

Finally, toddlers who regard meals as a nice enterprise in a day full of nice enterprises have a big advantage over those for whom meals are the highlight and redeeming feature of an otherwise boring or unpleasant existence.

4

Preschoolers:
Three to Five Years
THE LITTLEST KIDS

Preschoolers want approval as much as they want their own way, thank heavens. Parents still have so much influence that helping a child grow into, or keep from acquiring, extra baby fat is easier now than it will ever be later on. Because a whole raft of normal, wholesome lifestyles can actually encourage too much weight gain, parents who want to help their preschooler need tools with which to analyze what's really going on. After all, many lifestyles are pretty sophisticated for Threes and Fours these days. There's a lot going on: friends, other adults, the concept of Girl and Boy, TV, videos, and often structured activities like preschool and lessons.

PRESCHOOLER FAT FACTS

- Most preschoolers gain about four and one-half pounds a year—that's about six ounces a month.
- Little boys normally show quite a decrease in amount of fat during this time; they change shape more than little girls do.
- Most preschoolers need between 1,300 and 1,800 calories a day. Their intake normally will vary enormously depending

---

on body build and activity and on what is served at each meal.

- Most preschoolers normally eat one good meal a day and the rest of the time "just pick."
- Given *regularly timed* meals and snacks of *nutritious* foods, most preschoolers will eat the amounts needed for their energy and growth needs without any need for adults to regulate quantities.
- Preschoolers should have fat limited to about 30 percent of their daily calories, or between 400 and 600 calories of fat daily.
- Food traps for preschoolers with a tendency to gain extra fat include fat-rich meals and snacks such as cheese and cold cuts, juice as a beverage, too much milk, and constant "munchies" of crackers and cookies.
- Preschoolers should be drinking about twelve ounces of milk daily for calcium needs. Most preschoolers do better on non-fat or 1% fat milk.
- Most popular juices contain either no or insignificant amounts of vitamins and minerals such as iron or calcium. For preschoolers with a tendency toward gaining extra fat, water is the beverage of choice.
- Preschoolers may not get as much exercise as parents assume they do. Many are very "project" oriented and spend lots of time on crafts. Others are devoted to TV or to imaginative play with dolls and superheroes that doesn't involve running or climbing. Little girls may start to find rough-and-tumble play with boys unpleasant, as each sex works out its manner of making and keeping friends.

Tiffany and Kayla are best buddies (as are their single mothers). And a good thing, too. If they didn't have each other, with whom would they play?

What other Fours regard a day without five changes of clothes as a day without sunshine?

*What other mothers have found their preschoolers at 10 P.M.
combing their Barbies' hair by the glow of the nightlight?*

Who else loves to fold clothing, just for the joy of folding?

(Oh! You mean they're not the only ones?)

Here is Kayla, climbing onto the exam table in her red peasant blouse, green plaid kilt with the safety pin missing, black tights, white Jellies, and her mother's sweatband around her waist like a belt.

She is joining Tiffany, whose ears I am examining.

Tiffany is wearing many layers. We start by removing the velvet cape, then the pink tutu, then the black turtleneck, and finally the flowered bathing suit. I agree that she can keep on her hat, a ski cap with snowflakes on a red background. (It is early June.) Kayla, in maternal fashion, folds each item (of course).

Kayla and Tiffany live around the block from each other. Their mothers are attractive women of appropriate weight. By report, both fathers are skinny. These little girls are picked up in the morning by one mother or the other and taken to the same preschool where they are in the same class. Whichever mother picks them up brings them identical breakfasts to eat in the car; the preschool serves both of them the same food; and after school they attend the same child-care center. More days than not the two families eat together. Most often, the two mothers cook a simple dinner.

Kayla is mostly arms and legs. The headband-belt fits comfortably, not snugly, around her waist.

Tiffany is mostly tummy. She has the kind of cheeks that kindly strangers must restrain the urge to pinch.

Does Tiffany eat a lot of snacks? Huge portions of food? Nope. So what's going on here? Genes? A mistake in paternity, perhaps, on the part of Tiffany's mother? Perhaps Dad was really—er, pudgy?

Nope again.

I've known them from birth. I've watched Tiffany gradually ascend the Weight for Height chart, from the 50th to the 75th to the 90th percentile; and today she is off the chart. Today, she is forty inches tall—average for just-turned-Four—and she weighs forty-four pounds. The average-build little girl of forty inches weighs thirty-five pounds. If Tiffany weighed forty pounds, she would weigh more than 90 percent of little girls her height. At forty-four pounds, she weighs more than 99.9 percent of them.

Tiffany's Growth Charts

How Long Will It Take Her to "Slim Down"?

HEIGHT FOR AGE

Today, Tiffany is four. She is forty inches tall. To find out how tall she is compared with other little girls her age, we will use the Height for Age chart. We find her age, four years, along the bottom of the chart. We find her height, forty inches, along the scale on the left-hand side. We draw lines from both points and see where they intersect, and where that point of intersection is in relation to the percentile lines.

We see that Tiffany's height for age mark is right on the line marked 50, or the 50th percentile. This means that if you lined up Tiffany with 100 little girls age four, 50 would be taller and 50 would be shorter than Tiffany.

WEIGHT FOR HEIGHT

To see how much plumper Tiffany is than other little girls who are as tall as she is, we find her height in inches on the scale at the bottom. Then we find her weight in pounds, on either one of the scales at the sides. We draw lines from each point and see where they intersect. They do so at about two little boxes above the 95th percentile line.

This means that if you lined up Tiffany with 100 little girls forty inches tall, not one would weigh more than Tiffany does. All would weigh less. In fact, half of these normal, healthy little girls of Tiffany's height would weigh thirty-five pounds or less. Tiffany is nine pounds over.

Growing into the Extra Baby Fat

We want to help Tiffany grow into her weight. How long will it take for Tiffany to grow into her extra baby fat?

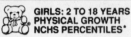

Name **TIFFANY**   Record #

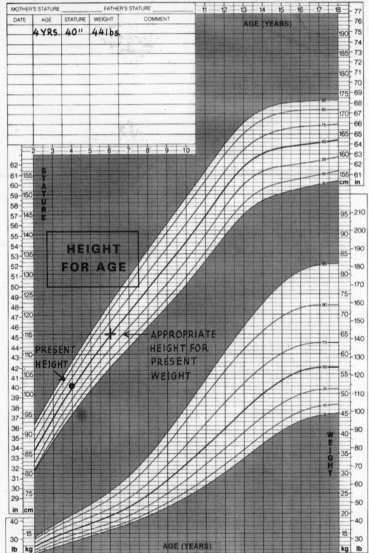

DATE	AGE	STATURE	WEIGHT	COMMENT
	4 YRS.	40"	44 lbs.	

HEIGHT
FOR AGE

PRESENT
HEIGHT

APPROPRIATE
HEIGHT FOR
PRESENT
WEIGHT

*Adapted from: Hamill PVV, Drizd TA, Johnson CL, Reed RB, Roche AF, Moore WM. Physical growth: National Center for Health Statistics percentiles. AM J CLIN NUTR 32:607-629, 1979. Data from the National Center for Health Statistics (NCHS), Hyattsville, Maryland.

© 1982 Ross Products Division, Abbott Laboratories

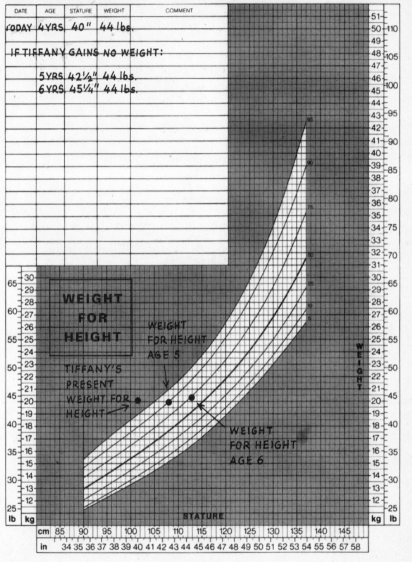

GIRLS: PREPUBESCENT PHYSICAL GROWTH NCHS PERCENTILES*

Name **TIFFANY**

Record #_____

DATE	AGE	STATURE	WEIGHT	COMMENT
TODAY	4YRS	40"	44 lbs.	
IF TIFFANY GAINS NO WEIGHT:				
	5YRS	42½"	44 lbs.	
	6YRS	45¼"	44 lbs.	

WEIGHT FOR HEIGHT

WEIGHT FOR HEIGHT AGE 5

TIFFANY'S PRESENT WEIGHT FOR HEIGHT

WEIGHT FOR HEIGHT AGE 6

STATURE

51214 09893WB
(0.05)/JUNE 1994

LITHO IN USA

If Tiffany gains no weight at all for one year but grows in height at the same rate, at age five she will be forty-two and one-half inches tall and weigh, still, forty-four pounds. When we put these numbers on the Weight for Height chart, we find that Tiffany has slimmed down to the 90th percentile.

If Tiffany again gains no weight at all for yet another year, at six she will be forty-five and one-quater inches tall and weigh, still, forty-four pounds. This puts her right back at the 50th percentile! Hooray!

If Tiffany slows her weight gain, rather than halting it, she can still grow into the extra baby fat. It will just take longer. But if she continues to gain more than the weight expected from year to year, her babyfat problems are likely to increase.

●●●

Kayla is also forty inches tall, and she weighs thirty-eight pounds. Next to Tiffany, she looks skinny. But Kayla weighs more than 75 percent of little girls of her height.

So which mother is worried? Kayla's, of course. Kayla is a "bad eater" and "eats like a bird." Kayla's mom agrees that Tiffany is "a little chubby." Tiffany's mother has a suspicion that Tiffany is a bit on the chunky side, but "it goes with her personality. And she has a big build."

I am the only person in the room concerned about Tiffany. I'm concerned on several scores, all of which pretty much sum up the preschool chubbiness dilemma.

But let me make it very clear that Tiffany is not fat because she binge eats or gets a lot of candy or french fries or chips or soft drinks, or because she watches too much TV. (You cannot fold a TV set, comb its hair, or change its clothes. What good is it.)

How did Tiffany become so chubby? Has her mother been doing something wrong? Restricted her exercise? Fed her all the wrong foods? Not at all.

Tiffany has gained this weight very gradually since infancy. She is the classic example of the child whose daily energy intake exceeds by just a little bit her daily energy expenditure. Her fatness is not due to anything abnormal that we could step in and correct just like that. I can't do something as easy as saying, "Don't force her to drink five glasses of whole milk a day!" or "Turn off that TV set! Get rid of it!"

Tiffany's activity level reflects a perfectly valid and typical play style for a little girl her age. It is hard to see how to get her to exercise more.

This is an age for very intense gender-oriented play. On the preschool playground, Tiffany and Kayla mostly push each other on the tire swing, play with their dolls in the big net hammock, and pretend to be princesses, brides, and (I am quite serious) lawyers with briefcases.

At home on the weekends the little girls don't pedal tricycles or bikes with training wheels; their neighborhood is too hilly. The climbing structures at the park are Boy Territory; I need say no more. It is a rare day that either of them is sweaty and out of breath for more than a couple of minutes.

Often, their mothers put Kayla and Tiffany (wearing helmets) on the backs of their bikes and go for a picnic. Sometimes, the little girls will bring their dolls and crayoning things to the courts while their mothers play tennis. In the winter, it is a struggle to get on all the stuff: snowsuit, boots, hats, scarves. Two minutes of making "snow angels" and both little girls are "frozen" and have to come in to pee. In the summer, the pool is scary with many splashing big kids. Both mothers work, and neither is comfortable having someone else watch the little girls at a swim lesson.

Tiffany is a calm soul. She does not fidget, nor does she bounce.

Here is Kayla, squirming around on the exam table. She hops down to get the Kleenex box, climbs up again, drops one of her Jelly slippers, climbs down to get it, hops around getting it back on her foot, tries various ways of reascending the exam table, and then sits there jiggling one foot and scratching her back. Tiffany, in the meantime, has peacefully sat. "Kayla, do you think you could sit still for just a few minutes?" Tiffany's mother says defeatedly.

Tiffany eats what most parents and pediatricians would regard as an amazingly healthy diet.

She drinks sixteen ounces of low-fat milk a day. She has a hard-boiled egg or cream cheese on a bagel and a container of orange juice for breakfast; a cup of apple juice and a graham cracker or two for snack; a water-packed tuna sandwich with low-fat mayonnaise, an apple, and one Oreo cookie for a typical lunch; and maybe a serving of a casserole, a vegetable, and vanilla pudding and a Fig Newton for dessert.

But Tiffany eats all of it, every bit, every scrap, except the apple.

Whereas Kayla, in her mother's words, "just picks." She eats only half her morning bagel; half her sandwich, about three-quarters of her apple, and the filling of the Oreo cookie for lunch; and for dinner a third of the casserole, one bite of the vegetable, and only the stuffing of her Fig Newton. (Carefully picking off the cookie crust, she dips the fig part into her vanilla pudding as if it were a taco scooping up guacamole.)

Here are my concerns for Tiffany and—a bit—for Kayla.

First, Tiffany is already fat. This worries me because she is in the age group (from two to about ten) when children who are not obese do not make more fat cells. But children who are obese make more fat cells. These fat cells do not go away; they are there for life. And each little fat cell wants to feel good; it doesn't want to shrink. If Tiffany continues to make more and more fat cells, by the time she hits puberty and really starts to increase the number of fat cells, we'll have trouble: Tiffany's "set point" for how much weight feels good will be high. Now is the time to help Tiffany put the brakes on the creation of new fat cells. (This is discussed in the preface, too.)

Second, Tiffany already is chubby enough that she will require a long time to "slim down," even if she gains no weight whatsover as she grows in height.

If she stays at the 50th percentile for height, her forty-four pounds will start to be appropriate for her when she is forty-four inches tall, at Five and a Half. Even then, she may be a little chubby—weighing more than 75 percent of girls her height. If she continues to gain over the next years, even if her weight gain is very modest—say, two pounds a year—it will be still further

in the future that Tiffany achieves a "normal" weight for height.
But why be concerned about Kayla?

I am concerned that Tiffany's weight is actually contagious, and that Kayla is "catching" it. Here is my evidence.

• Kayla's mother thinks that Kayla looks thin in comparison with Tiffany. She thinks Kayla ought to weigh more. Also, in comparison with Tiffany, Kayla is unrewarding to prepare food for. This makes Kayla's mother coax and lure Kayla into taking one more bite or offering an Oreo as a reward if she cleans her plate.

• Kayla is distracting to have around. Adults tend to try to quiet her down. But it is not Kayla who is overly active: Tiffany just happens to be unusually quiet, and it is the comparison that adults notice.

• Any impulses Kayla might have for being more active or less gender-preoccupied are discouraged by her love—and children do love one another—for Tiffany. Tiffany is not likely to change her tastes in activity on her own, especially because the extra weight makes her huff and puff when she runs. And leaving Tiffany to play with the other children might well be seen by Kayla as a betrayal of friendship: yes, even at this age, and even more so as they grow.

• So Kayla (like Tiffany) isn't learning the playground skills, both physical and social, that will allow her to be more active as she gets into kindergarten and beyond.

Oddly enough, my next patient is Toby. Toby's parents are both way off the top line on the chubbiness scale. When I met with them for their prenatal visit, they had only one item on their agenda: They didn't want Toby to grow up chubby. They knew that a tendency to obesity can be inherited, but they also knew that there are lots of inherited tendencies that can be effectively overcome.

I made a bargain with them. I would guide them to help Toby stay "just right" for Toby, on two conditions: first, that they would allow me to do all the worrying; and second, that they would trust me to take their worries seriously. I told them I wouldn't "feed them a line" (Toby's father's words) that because Toby was healthy, they shouldn't worry about extra weight.

They are both here today with Toby, who has a nasty case of hand–foot–mouth virus. Toby, at three, looks wonderful (except for his infected hands, feet, and mouth). He is slightly padded, with a little curving tummy, but no jiggling or overlapping or dimpled fat. Even better, his parents have stopped worrying. We talk about keeping him well hydrated and taking fluids while his mouth hurts, but they don't show a glimmer of concern when I recommend sweet, soothing drinks.

Well, you already know about how Toby and his parents and I have managed his weight up until now: Just glance at the previous two chapters.

Tiffany, Kayla, and Toby are more alike than different when it comes to staying, or becoming, "just right" in weight.

THE GOAL

The overall goal for these years is to keep preschoolers feeling and acting like normal, adored, bright, witty, strong little kids, while at the same time finding ways to help chubby preschoolers grow into and stay in the "just right" range. These strategies must last for the long term. Ideally, each one should take very little time or money; should be as close as possible to invisible and unnoticeable in the life of the child and family; and should have the attribute of quickly becoming a habit you don't even have to think about.

THE CHALLENGE

Here is what makes this so tricky.

All the aspects of life that encourage excess chubbiness can seem like normal, desirable parts of preschool development. It takes an act of will to look at them differently. It means going against the cultural grain. It may mean revisiting one's own early childhood—what you, as a little girl or boy, found normal and delightful. It certainly means looking with new eyes at your child's lifestyle.

Often, changing a few of the rituals and expectations in a preschooler's life just slightly can make all the difference in the world. This may take a parental act of courage and commitment, but it's important to realize that these preschool years are particularly crucial for children like Tiffany, Kayla, and Toby.

After the preschool years, parents diminish as intimate forces in their children's lives. Friends, school, activities, the media, and the urge to become separate and individual start to take hold at five and a half or six. From then on, trying to change family patterns of any kind is hard, whether it's how the family shops, cooks, and eats; how they exercise together or separately; how they communicate about things that upset them; how they make requests or give orders; how they complain or praise.

So this is a very special time, and I urge parents to make the most of it.

THE ASSESSMENT

In looking at preschoolers, the trick is to remember that they are no longer babies but little kids. A too-chubby preschooler often looks not fat but like a slightly rounded two-year-old, with a protruding belly, a round face with soft features, and padded arms and legs. This can be very misleading. So when a preschooler has a double chin and fatty rolls that overlap the pants and chubby thighs that jiggle and fat that dimples like "cellulite," that preschooler is *well* over the "just right" range.

Even though parents may be aware of this, the eye can be fooled. Perhaps most of the preschoolers in a particular neighborhood or day-care center or community are very chubby; as a group, they just look round and cute. Or a family's history has included very hard times with not enough food, and a fat child is balm to the soul.

If you think or know that your preschooler is chubby and you find that you are worried about it—that you have a niggling concern, that you wish you could do something about it—there is probably a reason why. Perhaps there's a family history of chubbiness that turns into unhappy overweight or eating disorders in

certain individuals. Or, on the other hand, perhaps nobody at all in the family is chubby, and you are concerned about the fact that this little one is different.

You are right to be concerned:

- If a preschooler is above the 90th percentile on the Weight for Height chart.
- If you look at a preschooler's previous measurements and find that he or she is "crossing percentile lines." By this, I mean: Suppose that all the way up to the age of two years, Cherub's weight for height was in the 50th percentile. Then at age two and a half it was up almost to the 75th percentile, and at age three it is now at just below the 90th per-

centile. This is a definite trend signaling that something has changed in Cherub's food/activity balance starting after age two—and that it needs to be addressed.

• If a preschooler is showing signs of resisting and avoiding energetic activity or of using food to "fix" boredom, frustration, loneliness, or other unhappy feelings.

On the other hand, if your worry is not about the way a preschooler looks, acts, or plots out in the chart but rather about a strong family history of problems with overweight or eating disorders, you certainly need to discuss these worries with your pediatrician. You will feel much better with a promise that your pediatrician will keep a close eye on the situation, maybe even with measurements three times a year, and will do the worrying *for* you.

This examination should be done tactfully, with lots of play and without worry or disappointment or criticism communicated to the child. Any mention of fat, or of strategies to help a preschooler slim down, should be done without the young person around.

The only exception is if the preschooler has expressed worry or distress about being too chubby. Then the kind and appropriate response is to reassure him or her that being very chubby is the way some children grow, and that it is the job of doctors and parents to see that when preschooler becomes a big kid he or she won't be so chubby.

Preschoolers just love to know that something is a job, and to know whose job it is. They don't need to know how somebody else plans on performing that job, but if they ask, keep explanations simple. "By making all the food power go into growing and playing, not into making chubbiness" is a good answer.

Parents who are committed and kind in helping preschoolers maintain or slow down weight gain while growing in height can help make these years joyous and make such preschoolers feel good about themselves.

If preschoolers aren't so lucky, the coming years can be tough. By first grade, children are very polarized in terms of gender. They are much more conscious of, and critical of, physical differences. They watch and listen to their parents, to adults in the community, to TV and videos, and they copy what they absorb—and much of it can be mean and nasty. Children in elementary school who are overly chubby can take a licking.

At this age, the teasing of little boys isn't based on lack of athletic excellence. In fact, a little boy who is overly chubby may be only marginally less active and coordinated in preschoool and kindergarten and even in the early school years. In physical fights, he may even have the advantage: My good friend Manny developed a marvelous technique of sitting on an opponent's knees, facing backward, and removing the adversary's shoes, which he then wore on his own ears.

But an overly chubby preschooler *looks* different from the other boys. He may, like Buster, be quite macho in voice and style, but small daily problems will harass him. He waddles. He can't sit with his legs in certain positions. He can't scoot over enough to make room on the seat in the school bus; he can't wear the same kinds of clothes as the other boys; he may be self-conscious about taking off his shirt—mean children may refer to his "boobies."

A little girl who is overly chubby has a less predictable row to hoe. In some kindergartens and early grades, little girls are expected to be very "girly," playing with dolls and behaving in docile fashion, like Tiffany. In others, little girls are out on the playground or soccer field or hockey rink, learning to inline skate and surf and ski and ride a pony, learning to fight like the boys. In still others, little girls are expected to be obsessed with fashion and beauty—when they comb Barbie's hair by the nightlight, it's not with maternal concern. In still others, little girls are urged into the graceful arts: ballet, ice skating, child modeling. And finally, some little girls are true little mothers, asked by overwhelmed parents to take on the chores of housekeeping and caring for even younger siblings.

It all depends.

Loving parents can go out of their way to help the Busters and Tiffanies not only slim down but also make and keep friends during these years. They can help them learn skills and sports in which weight is no drawback—from magic tricks, yo-yos, and the ability to tell truly awful jokes to swimming and diving to camping and being conversant in nature lore. They can shield the Tiffanies from restricted female-only roles and both sexes from precociously competitive athletics. They can make their home a good one at which to visit.

Even with no one to help, some children do pretty well. A number of very overweight young children are such good friends to others, so much fun, so loyal, so possessed of such inborn confidence and imagination and kindness and guts that friends just gather around, and woe be to the person who teases or is mean.

But others (like any child who feels unliked and unappreciated) turn to behaviors that don't help them mature and that may get them into trouble: clowning, exaggerating, and lying; boasting and then perhaps stealing to make good the boast; bullying. Or they may turn inward and seemingly try to become invisible, never making an overture of friendship, volunteering an answer or a riddle or a joke, finding a seat alone rather than assuming the right, or asking the privilege, to share.

But here's something terrific. Several studies have shown that despite the harrassment and embarrasment that are often heaped on the very chubbies, self-esteem tends to stay high until adolescence. Sure, Chubby may be unhappy in first or fourth grade; but that unhappiness is experienced as external. Only in adolescence does it seem to become "I am unhappy because I am no good because I am too fat." There's lots of time for caring parents to help their preschooler enter adolescence with self-esteem intact.

Now, not all or even most very overweight preschoolers grow up to be obese adults. Only about 40 percent do. In my view, however, the statistic begs the question.

First, we don't know why 60 percent of overweight preschoolers do slim down. What happened in their lives? Was it luck, or someone's intervening? Did the children's metabolism just naturally change, destined by genes to do so? Did the children themselves take matters in hand?

Second, we don't know at what age they attained normal weight, and we don't know how life was for them during the years they quickly or slowly slimmed down.

Third, 40 percent is a number not to be sneezed at. That's a lot of children. And we can't predict whether an individual child will be in the 60 percent or the 40 percent.

Fourth, we should not be concerned exclusively with the health risks of the obese adult. We know there are health risks just from being a very overweight child. For instance, little girls may get stubborn vaginal infections. This is partly due to the fact that the thighs are so chubby that the vagina is kind of sealed off and is hard to wash and harder to keep dry. Chubby children with asthma can get into breathing trouble sooner.

Only very rarely should even the chubbiest preschooler *lose* weight, and then only with close supervision by the pediatrician and by a nutritionist specializing in children. Losing weight at this age is difficult and unkind and can even be dangerous. Far more likely to succeed and promising to be safe is growing into the extra weight over the next months or years.

How long will that take?

A Four who is markedly overweight is going to take a long time to slim down even in the best of all worlds. Even gaining hardly any weight a year, a Four, for example, is not going to be close to friends in body shape until kindergarten or even first grade. If slimming down is slower, Four can look ahead to spending the early years of grade school overly plump.

This is calculated by using the growth charts. Assume that your preschooler will grow in height along the same curve he or she has been on. Then find when, on that height curve, the present weight will fall at somewhere between the 50th and the 75th percentiles.

This calculation won't tell you how long the "slimming down" will really take. It will tell you only how long "slimming down" will take if the preschooler gains *no* weight between now and then. It is the *minimum* amount of time in which you should expect "slimming down."

Once you know the minimum time "slimming down" would take, you can then have the pediatrician calculate how much longer it will take if the preschooler gains, say, only two pounds a year until the weight is appropriate for the height.

It's a good idea for the truly Much Too Chubby preschooler to have height and weight measurements about every three months. First, you want to make sure that height is proceeding along its established curve. Second, you want to make sure that the preschooler is not losing weight. Third, you want to see whether you are staying in the range of weight gain you had planned: perhaps two pounds a year, which comes out to about a half-pound gain at each visit. If things aren't going well, your pediatrician will help you figure out why, without making you feel guilty. If they are, your pediatrician will be all smiles and say wonderful things that make you feel great.

Now you won't be constantly casting a jaundiced eye on your preschooler's chubby, lovely little body, hoping to see something happening. You'll be calm and fond and full of pats and hugs, without qualms.

THE PLAN

A plan that works is one that will help change the balance of energy in and energy expended on a daily, long-term basis. This plan must be as easy on the whole family as possible and shouldn't leave the preschooler feeling deprived of treats and goodies, or parents and loving adults feeling deprived of being nurturing.

Remember that you are looking at a probably very subtle imbalance between calories going in the mouth and calories being expended in activity. A difference of fifty of those calories a day, every day, over the years from one to three may have added ten extra pounds, for instance.

Remember, the key word is *subtle*. Don't dream of suddenly forcing Four into Pee Wee Hockey, if such a thing exists; or of depriving Three of her afternoon snack.

Exercise

Many people believe that Threes and Fours are just naturally full of energy and spend their days running around all the time. Well, some are and do. Some aren't and don't. And some are full of energy but have no opportunity to run.

For the Too Chubby Three or Four, exercise and activity can be complicated beyond belief.

First, there's temperament and interest—witness Tiffany.

She is a bit like Ferdinand the Bull in the story by Munro Leaf; she just wants to sit and smell the flowers. Montana, one of her preschool classmates, occupies the other extreme of the bell-shaped curve. He jiggles and bounces and scratches, even when he's sitting in circle time at preschool ("Even when he's asleep!" says his mother).

Second, there are gender games.

Threes and Fours are highly gender-conscious. Kayla and Tiffany and four other little girls play house, dolls, and lawyers and push one another on the tire swing, and they occasionally indulge in bursts of running around giggling. Sometimes they play with toy trucks in the sandbox.

Montana and the rest of the boys are dashing about, riding wheeled things, finding squishy and odd things, pretending to shoot one another with anything that can look like a gun (toy guns are forbidden), falling down and leaping up, crawling through the play tunnel, climbing up the ladders, attacking one another, throwing balls, smashing things, digging things, and chasing the girls—especially the three little girls who don't play with Kayla and Tiffany.

These three little girls really do play on the expensive playground equipment, and not just the tire swing and the hammock. They climb the slide endlessly and pump on the swings and turn somersaults on the mats and jump on the trampoline. (Warning: The American Academy of Pediatrics has issued a statement that trampoline use *of any kind* is dangerous because of the risk of spinal cord injuries.) By the time preschool is over, they are dirty and sweaty.

Third, there's an enormous variation in enforced "down time."

A day-care group that has to accompany the day-care parent on errands—especially frequent doctor's visits or tasks related to the adult's other interests or business—spends a great deal of time unable to do much except sit and punch one another, crayon, yell, and eat.

Children in a preschool or day-care center located in an area with Weather most of the year—we don't have Weather in San Diego, but if you have it you know what it is—may get very little running around, too. Either they have to come in to pee as soon as they get dressed and outside; or they have to stay indoors. And indoors may well be too confining, or too full of quieter activities, or too crowded, or governed by adults too disinclined toward noise and fuss, to allow running about.

Moreover, many Threes and Fours spend their weekends in car pools, driven by parents for the benefit of older siblings.

And a number of Threes and Fours spend their afternoons and weekends indoors for safety reasons, either because their neighborhoods are dangerous or because the person in charge of them—perhaps an older sibling or a nanny who isn't comfortable in the local culture or language—isn't able to watch them well enough out in the big world.

Most Too-Chubby preschoolers contend with at least one of these factors: temperament, pressure to engage in gender-appropriate activities that are inactive, or lots of "down time."

ANALYZING ACTIVITY

Usually, analyzing activity takes just a pencil and paper and the right attitude. You are not doing this to suffer guilt or to spread blame. You are trying to figure out where in a preschooler's day you can add at least twenty minutes of sweaty running-around activity that is so much fun that it will turn into a daily habit.

Looking to the future, you are trying to develop outlook, aptitudes, and skills in your preschooler, so that later on Three or Four will have lots of play and sports options and will feel comfortable in the elementary school playground.

Here are some suggestions. You will come up with many more.

TEMPERAMENTALLY NOT ACTIVE

Threes and Fours who are watchers, thinkers, tinkerers, imaginers, or crafters can spend hours and hours without moving faster than a stroll. You can't force them to run about and climb things, and very rarely can an adult lure them into such "boring" activities.

And gimmicky ideas, like designing treasure hunts, work only sporadically. Here are some suggestions.

• Hire a seven- to nine-year-old playmate of the same sex to play with the preschooler half an hour a school day and an hour each weekend day. Most Threes and Fours idolize children this age. Make it a condition of employment that much of the time must be spent playing actively. Check for dirt and sweatiness. The hitch: An adult must be close by, strenuous safety rules are vital, and the pla mate must be responsible and mature and *nice*. And need the money.

• Find a way for the preschooler to walk daily. Tiffany's and Kayla's mothers decided to get up twenty minutes early and drive together to about five blocks from the preschool. One mother had the little girls walk, skip, hop, run like horses, and dance to school, while the other "drove shotgun."

You may well come to cherish these walks. Coming home, if you have the energy, do the same thing—park, walk to the site, and walk back with your preschooler.

• Engage the preschooler in helping with tasks that expend energy. Usually children with this temperament love one-to-one adult attention, especially if the task is a gender-related. Tiffany turned out to love helping wash the car, paying special attention to polishing the hubcaps. Then there's shoveling snow, raking leaves, polishing windows. The "reward" need only be praise.

• Search for a day-care center or preschool that structures running-around time into the day. Most do not; they allow free play and choices but have no structured time. Yet Threes and Fours are very interested in preserving the schedule of each day, and if it is time to run three times around the play yard, they'll do it, even in the snow.

INVESTED IN GENDER ROLE PLAYING

Little girls who are "invested in gender role playing" play the quieter Girl Games. This is so endearing, and clearly so much fun, that it's hard to intervene. But there's a reason to do so besides the considerations of "slimming down" and being comfortable later on in playground and sports situations.

Whenever we discuss eating, and weight, and chubbiness, and slimming down, there is a haunting, scary shadow in the background: the shadow of eating disorders, especially of anorexia nervosa. And we know that one of the features of anorexia nervosa is that it thrives when a young girl doesn't have a healthy, well-developed sense of self.

We can't endow children with self-esteem. They have to earn it. Much of self-esteem comes from feeling that you've done a good job at something: that you faced a challenge and solved it yourself. That helps you be brave enough to take some risks and get more self-esteem.

The activities in which it is very clear that one has faced a challenge, solved it, and done a good job, really do divide down traditional gender lines. That is, if preschoolers stay right on those traditional lines, little girls don't get much of this.

Little and big boys know when they've learned to pitch a good ball or pedal the trike faster and get to the pole and "win," or when they've gotten the better of someone in a physical contest— grabbing the toy, pushing someone down, pulling her pigtail, when they've crossed the monkey bars or gotten up on the skateboard or kicked the ball into the net. And on and on.

Watch the Threes and Fours at play. How do little girls playing gender games know when they've done a good job? That the mudpies are cooked well, or that Barbie's outfit is fabulous, or that baby doll is well fed and cared for, or that the rainbow has beautiful colors? There's no endpoint or specific goal. They know because it satisfies them deep inside—or because somebody else admires their work. Or doesn't.

There's a big difference.

So I do urge you to widen the play experiences of the intensely gender-playing little girl. Here are some suggestions; again, you will think of many more.

• Ease into it with such girl-associated but active play as dance or gymnastics. Anything with a special costume is likely to be a hit. Karate, anyone?

• Hire a seven- to ten-year-old girl to play with the pre-schooler for half an hour a weekday and an hour on week-ends. Ask her to teach your preschooler how to throw and kick a ball, ride a trike, run fast. Most female preschoolers are enthralled with such older girls to imitate.

• If you are her mother or aunt or grandmother or other loving female adult, model being physically active and en-joying it. Don't admit to her that you may be exercising for ulterior motives, like cellulite; let her believe that it is a fun, feminine activity.

• If you are her father or uncle or grandfather or other loving male adult, let her hear you admiring women's accomplish-ments, not only in sports but also in other nontraditionally female activities. And praise her and brag about her in her hearing when she accomplishes something along those lines.

TOO MUCH DOWN TIME

Having too much down time is the toughest of all and may require draconian measures. First, go over the activities of a typical week from the preschooler's point of view. How much driving around, waiting around, sitting around, lying down?

If the preschooler is at the day-care center or at preschool, don't assume anything, and don't take on faith any answers you get to questions: Visit several times and see what is going on. Listen for clues: If the preschooler seems extremely involved with and up to date on several morning or afternoon TV shows or videos, you may be justified in assuming that a couple of hours of TV are on the day-care or preschool agenda.

Threes and Fours often need a half hour to an hour of quiet time in the afternoon, but they rarely need a nap. A regularly scheduled nap, or quiet time that is enforced and lasts more than an hour, is pretty suspect. If your Three or Four can't get to sleep until after 8 o'clock and comes home from day care or preschool very refreshed and very clean, you may have discovered the reason why.

Second, if any of this rings a bell, you need to change either the preschool or day-care center's philosophy—or the preschool or day-care center.

As for the weekend driving around as a tag-along in a car pool, perhaps Three or Four could join an active playgroup—perhaps formed with the younger siblings of the carpool gang. (Besides getting more activity, there's another benefit: The preschooler will be deprived of learning and imitating all kinds of undesirable vocalizations from the carpool gang and its driver.)

Nutrition

In middle-class America, eating is about choosing.

Preschoolers need from the bottoms of their hearts to be able to make choices. And when I say make a choice, this is a very special action.

- First, the choice must be a real one, between two equally attractive alternatives.
- Second, it must be a free one. Once an adult says, "You choose!" it's not fair to make a face or a comment that implies, "Uh-oh, you made the wrong choice."
- Third, ideally the choice should be recognized in a positive way. But this is very delicate. Just as the adult oughtn't to say, "You made the wrong choice," it isn't fair to say "Ah, good, you made the right choice." The whole point about choosing is confirming one's ability to choose! It oughtn't to be a guessing game.

To recognize a choice, then, a good way is simply to name it. "I see you chose the red peasant blouse today." "I see you decided to have a muffin instead of the bread." "I see you chose Frosted Flakes instead of Froot Loops." In a positive, upbeat voice, of course, and with a smile. You might then say something like, "You're learning to make choices. It's fun to see what you choose."

Delightfully, several studies now have shown that making their own choices about how much of each food they eat helps young children stay and become their "just right" weight. Over a few days' time, they will pick out the right number of calories and choose food that gives them their recommended requirements.

Now that is terrific, but it's not the whole story.

The whole story comes in several parts.

• The loving adult decides which foods go on the table. The child decides how much of each to eat. Coaxing, urging, expressing joy or disappointment about a preschooler's choices will backfire.

• But when you offer the foods that a preschooler is to choose from, you have to be fair. Threes and Fours, like everybody else, enjoy sweet, fatty, and salty foods and tend to choose them over other foods. In other words, such foods become habitual, addicting; they aren't "chosen" at all. If you offer a meal that contains both potato chips and beets, guess which one you'll have lots of left.

• The meals that you are serving for breakfast, lunch, and dinner are probably just fine as they are. However, there are a few problem areas, as they say, to watch out for.

• Having a daily dessert that is a pastry or ice cream is a hard habit to break and one that nobody needs. If you are going to help your preschooler avoid this habit in the future, start now. A sweet end to a meal is always nice, but there are alternatives to traditional sweets. For instance, you could serve a nonfat milk-based pudding or a piece of fruit (if it's cut fancily, like a sushi-meal orange, or an apple with a raisin face, that makes it special) or aspartane-sweetened gelatin. Or water-packed fruit cocktail, if you don't mind watching your preschooler sort it all into little heaps of pineapple, grape, apple. . . .

• If you are using cream or butter with a liberal hand, or frying things regularly, have a heart-to-heart talk with yourself. Make it a present to your preschooler to learn to do things a little more healthfully.

• Beware of catsup and mayonnaise. They are highly "addicting," and some children, once introduced to the stuff, won't eat *anything* unless the food is doused in one or the other or both. If adults are already addicted, try serving catsup in a bowl—not a bottle—and serving it to oneself as if it were a food, and without any particular enthusiasm; maybe with a little dutiful sigh. Offer it to your preschooler with the exact same manner as you offer the beets and rutabaga.

• Serve small portions. A good rule: Each portion should be no more than the size of a playing card, with three or four such servings on the plate. Let the preschooler choose which three or four foods go on the plate. If the preschooler wants only *one* food, give only one card-sized portion. When that is finished, offer each of the foods on the table again, but don't insist that any be taken. Just be thankful that the one food your preschooler has chosen is relatively low in fat and sugar and has some redeeming nutritional value—because each choice is a healthful one at your table.

• If your preschooler wants seconds or thirds of anything, keep those portions half the size of the initial portion. Don't insist that everything else be eaten, or even tasted, before giving the additional helping. Because dessert (as noted previously) is as nutritious as any other part of the meal, it's fine to have seconds of that, too.

• If the preschooler refuses a particular food meal after meal, that's fine. Make no comment. At nonmealtimes, however, feel free to indulge in subtle propaganda: "When Uncle Bert was driving race cars, he always said that eating rutabaga made his eyesight sharper so he could go faster." And, if your preschooler does finally try the refused food, of course, follow up: "Why, Toby, I can't believe you can see that tiny little airplane up in the sky. It must be because you ate your rutabaga and that made your eyes so bright and sharp."

WHAT HELPS

IN GENERAL

- Keep repeating: Adults decide what, where, and when to eat. Preschoolers decide how much. Pretend a total lack of interest in how much. If a preschooler is above the "just right" range, address other issues: exercise, fat content, munchies, and juice.
- Involve your preschooler in planning menus and in buying, making, and serving food. There's nothing like the feeling that you've chosen, stirred, and judged the seasoning on the rutabaga to make you want to eat it.
- Expect and demand reasonable manners. A few idiosyncrasies make this more fun, for instance a toast in the middle of the meal. Preschoolers love to clink glasses and then clap and shout.

WITH PLANNING MEALS

- Have something chewy (but not choke-threatening) at each meal.
- Foods you can sort are time consuming and interesting. Water-packed fruit cocktail is great.
- If you are going to serve something that you know preschoolers don't like, serve at the same meal one thing preschoolers like pretty well and one thing you think they would like if they gave it a chance.
- Explore foods of other cultures that you eat with your fingers or do something interesting with: dip it or pinch it or whatever. Just don't dip it in butter or mayonnaise.

WITH EATING

- If a preschooler always monopolizes the conversation, bring a "talking doll" to the table. Whoever has the talking doll can talk for a few minutes and then has to pass it to somebody else. "Time to pass the doll" is much more polite and effective than "Do you think you could just be quiet for a few minutes?"

> • If a parent does something rude or disgusting at the table, he or she has to apologize and leave the table for a minute of Time Out. (Same with a preschooler.)
>
> • If anybody truly, truly can't find anything appealing in a meal, there is one alternative that is easy to fix and reasonably healthful. Ideally, this should not be something "addicting" like peanut butter and jelly but something edible and unexciting, like nutritious cereal (not very sugary) with (nonfat or 1%) milk and fruit.

Milk

If your preschooler is drinking whole milk or lowfat milk, you can cut a large proportion of the daily calories by switching to 1% fat or nonfat milk.

No preschooler needs whole milk, and no overly chubby preschooler needs low-fat milk. (The difference in fat and calories between whole and 2% milk is truly minimal.)

If an overly chubby preschooler takes happily to "blue milk", by all means go to skim, nonfat milk. If he or she thinks it is disgusting, try 1% (extra-lite) or, if you can get away with it, half 1% and half nonfat milk.

How many calories then disappear?

If you go from whole to nonfat skim milk, you will cut down 67 calories for every cup (8 ounces) of milk. If a preschooler averages 16 ounces a day, that's a reduction of 134 calories a day.

If you go from whole to 1% milk, you will cut down 55 calories a cup. If a preschooler averages 16 ounces a day, that's a reduction of 110 calories a day.

If you go from low-fat 2% milk to 1% milk, you will cut 19 calories a cup. If a preschooler averages 16 ounces a day, that's a reduction of 38 calories. If you go from low-fat 2% to nonfat milk, that's a reduction of 31 calories per cup, or 62 calories a day.

Chocolate skim milk is fine for a treat but runs the risk of making a preschooler get used to "sweet milk" rather than "milky milk." Also, rather than satisfy the urge for chocolate, it may inspire a bit of a craving.

No preschooler drinks the same amount of milk every day. Most of the time, though, this amount varies only slightly. If so, how nice for you.

But sometimes the intake varies crazily: One day it's four ounces, the next twenty-eight, the third twelve. What you want to do is to figure out the daily average. If your preschooler follows this pattern, my suggestion is to estimate it over a week's time, just jotting down your estimate on a piece of paper attached by a magnet to the refrigerator. Then take into account milk drunk on a regular basis at day care or at preschool. When you ask the adults, be sure to sound friendly and not inquisitional—just curious.

An average daily amount of sixteen ounces of milk will give a preschooler about the daily needed calcium and about half the daily needed protein. But most Threes and Fours eat enough cheese, yogurt, or other sources of calcium that you don't need that much. For most, twelve ounces a day as an average is usually just fine: sixteen ounces one day, eight ounces another, twelve ounces another.

If a preschooler averages 24 ounces of whole milk a day and you drop to 16 ounces of nonfat skim milk a day, you have just dropped 291 calories a day.

If you've gone to 1% milk, you have just dropped 267 calories a day.

Food

MEALS

Breakfast is a "goodbye" meal for many Threes and Fours heading off to day care or preschool. It's kind, and helps keep eating from becoming a substitute for attention, if breakfast isn't too rushed. It's fine if a preschooler wants exactly the same thing every morning. Or, on the other hand, it's fine if anybody wants to interject a spark of humor into the meal: There is nothing wrong with a leftover chicken leg, taco, or piece of pizza for breakfast. Chocolate nonfat milk is fine.

Try to get in a source of vitamin C: three ounces of orange or grapefruit juice or cranberry juice cocktail will do it. If you must, apple juice fortified with vitamin C and iron can be served as part of breakfast, but not as a thirst quencher.

If your preschooler can't be content with any of the choices offered for breakfast, the issue is not about food. It's about being too rushed, not getting enough morning attention and hugging, having some doubts about separating from the family to go off into the world. Don't get into a fight about it; say, "I can see that you are having a hard time this morning. I will fix you a little peanut butter and jelly sandwich to eat on the way, and we will make sure that we have more time together in the morning before we say goodbye."

Lunch is usually an easy meal emotionally. It's not fraught with separation anxiety, and ideally it is construed by the preschooler as a mere interruption in an interesting day.

The only nutritional concern about lunch is the tendency to pack the meal with fats: processed cheese, cold cuts, hot dogs, ham. Excellent alternatives are organic peanut butter (not the fatty whipped kind) and jelly, water-packed tuna, low-fat yogurt, fruit, lean chicken, hard-boiled eggs, crackers, muffins, gelatin with fruit, and low-fat soups.

A cookie or two in a packed lunch makes sense—much better now than at dinner. A preschooler will see other children having them and may feel deprived if he or she has none. Learning to trade is a fine preschool skill, as is learning how to eat the filling of the Fig Newton but not the crust—or vice versa.

Dinner, very often, is the only meal everybody in the family eats more or less together. And it is also a meal at which most "just right" and some chubby preschoolers eat practically nothing. Alternatively, some Threes and Fours come home ravenous and irritable and can't wait until dinner.

Either of these scenarios can lead to woe.

I suggest some ground rules:

• Don't make any lifestyle changes that lead to even more problems. If you are used to serving Hamburger Helper, or frozen macaroni and cheese, or even fast food for dinner, don't throw yourself into a panic of guilt and resentment by trying to make healthful casseroles. Probably your preschooler isn't eating much at dinner anyway. Just try to follow the other recommendations—about exercise, milk, juice, snacks, and lunch—and let dinner stay the same. Unless you're used to a rich dessert every single night. That, I'd change.

• Cater to the irritable and ravenous preschooler by serving a snack, or even an early dinner if yours will be much later, as soon as he or she gets home. After the snack, a fifteen-minute "down time," one on one with Three or Four, can make the rest of the evening much happier.

• Enlist your preschooler in helping with dinner. This starts a sense of ownership about the food on the table and is a nice incentive to behave well at the meal.

• Don't hover or criticize or even notice what *anyone* is eating or not eating. Not a sibling or your spouse or your roommate or a grandparent, much less the preschooler.

• A rule: Nobody is allowed to complain out loud or make horrible faces about the food on the table. You can enforce this by sheer parental authority or by a minute of Time Out if you need to. If you have to use Time Out, let it be a parent who gets punished first.

JUICE

Juice as a part of a meal or snack is fine, especially if it is a citrus juice with natural vitamin C or a fortified juice of any kind with iron or vitamin C or A added. Juice as a beverage for the quenching of thirst is a problem. At fifteen calories an ounce, the daily total from juice can be ridiculous. Moreover, the constant infusion of sugar can make for cavities in teeth and, as well, produce diarrhea. But the real problem is that the message conveyed is that water is not a valued beverage because it isn't sweet. That is a hard, ingrained message to counteract later on, when the alternative drinks include sodas and alcohol.

SNACKS

The thing about snacks is that they're habit forming. If you are used to having, say, a Milky Way bar at 4:30, or an apple at 2 o'clock, or whatever, you will truly miss it when you don't get it. If you are used to your day-care grownup handing out small items to eat all day long—crackers, raisins, sunflower seeds—a day without munchies will seem like deprivation.

You can have nutritious snacks that are either high in calories or low in calories.

You can have empty-calorie snacks that are either high in calories or low in calories. Either one may have a high number or a low number of fat calories.

So there are four problems here.

• How much impact does a particular habitual snack have on total daily calories? (I am not talking about a once-in-a-while cookie. I am talking about the every-day-after-we-get-up-from-quiet-time-we-have-the-same-exact-thing ritual.)
• If we are talking all-day-long, handout munchies, how many calories do they add up to?
• Is any of this snacking nutritionally desirable? That is, do any of these snack foods give the preschooler something not gotten elsewhere in the diet?
• How many fat calories are these daily, ritualized snacks and munchies contributing?

Nobody, I am convinced, gets as broad a picture of typical snacks as do pediatricians. Here is a breakdown of popular snacks and munchies that I see.

SNACKS MOST PARENTS BELIEVE ARE WHOLESOME

TWELVE ANIMAL CRACKERS (half a box): 140 calories, with 35 fat calories. No calcium, vitamins, or iron. One gram of protein.

FOUR ARROWROOT CRACKERS: 150 calories, with 40 of them fat calories. Four percent of the daily iron requirement. No vitamins or other minerals.

APPLE JUICE: 90 calories (four-ounce container), all from sugar. No fat. No vitamins, no iron, no calcium, no other minerals.

HALF A CUP OF SEEDLESS RAISINS: 215 calories, no fat. A little vitamin C and a little iron, probably well absorbed.

TWO PLAIN GRAHAM CRACKERS: 107 calories, with 27 fat calories. A little calcium (about 10 mg).

SUNFLOWER SEEDS (Beware choking!): 190 calories (one-quarter of a cup), with 140 of them from fat. (An excellent source of vitamin E and magnesium, and a small amount of iron.) But I wouldn't trust anybody under age five to eat these safely.

TWO FIG NEWTONS: 110 calories, 20 of them fat; a small amount of iron.

ONE POP TART: 200 calories, 40 of them fat; provides 10 percent of the daily requirement of B vitamins and iron.

SNACKS EVERYBODY KNOWS AREN'T WHOLESOME

TWO CHOCOLATE CHIP COOKIES: 94 calories, with 36 fat calories.

THREE OREOS: 160 calories, 60 of them fat.

FIFTY-FIVE TINY GOLDFISH CRACKERS: 140 calories, with 50 from fat. But they also give a little calcium, B vitamins, and iron.

I want to stress: It's not the occasional snack I am talking about. I myself just ate fifty-five goldfish crackers while writing the above. (I counted them out to see what they look like in a sandwich-sized Baggie: They make a layer about one and one-half inches high.) And I feel just fine. The only problem is, the rest of the box is sitting here, calling to me.

Preschoolers, however, are very much creatures of habit, and so are the loving adults who run day-care centers and preschools.

But it's pretty clear that a 10 A.M. "wholesome" snack of, say, one Pop Tart, and another 2 P.M. "wholesome" snack of, say, two graham crackers and a cup of juice, are going to add up on a daily basis.

Strategy

First, I suggest that you insist on no "munchies" at all. Doling out raisins or fishy crackers or whatever at frequent intervals all day long without regard to either need or desire is a truly bad habit. First, it becomes just that: a habit. Second, it's bad for the teeth. It's bad even if the munchies aren't sugary. It's not sugar that causes tooth decay; it's the acid that bathes the teeth every single time you eat. If you're a preschooler nibbling all day long, that's a lot of acid.

Second, I would talk with the preschooler's other loving adults about what snacks to offer. An ideal plan would be to give at each snack a little bit—maybe two ounces—of the daily milk quota, plus a snack that preschoolers like but that isn't "off the chart" in terms of calories and fat.

Cheerios are great. Frosted Flakes are great. See the Appendix for other snack ideas. But don't be fooled into thinking that foods advertised as "wholesome" necessarily contain any vitamins or minerals at all, or any other ingredient that makes them a vital or even valid part of a child's diet.

For a summary of snacks, see the Appendix.

THE MORAL OF THE STORY

Threes and Fours are determined to figure out the world and their role in it. Much of this figuring out has to do with how you act and play as a boy or a girl, with how well you can climb and explore and master skills, and with how predictable—and solvable—your daily life is.

Helping the too-chubby or at-chubby-risk preschooler means understanding this point of view and taking measures to make the preschooler feel successful and adventurous. It means setting clear and consistent limits and offering meaningful choices. It means preserving regular one-to-one time with your preschooler and letting Three or Four know that you find him or her absolutely charming. Feeling liked is just as important as feeling loved.

It's not just about weight: It's about lifestyle. And it's not just about now, it's about the coming years, as well.

5

School-age Kids: Five to Puberty

WE ARE STILL THE CUTE ONES!

Growing into extra baby fat is possible up until puberty, but it becomes more tricky the longer you wait to intervene, especially for girls. Girls who are extra chubby going into puberty are not likely to shoot up into their weight; the hormones of puberty encourage **more** laying down of fat. Boys are far more likely to slim down after puberty. However, the most important goal for kids is not to "slim down" but to feel great about themselves: competent, in charge, respected, and—you guessed it—**cute.** What helps most is finding ways to help kids make healthy choices in exercise, nutrition, and lifestyle. Restricting food portions and prescribing weight-loss drugs and liquid diets are useless, and the last two are dangerous. Nagging, sarcasm, teasing, and indeed anything that overemphasizes food and fat will backfire: Not only will the kid gain more weight, but the whole family will be miserable. Kidhood is supposed to be fun. If fat is getting in the way of fun, get help beyond this book!

SCHOOL-AGE FAT FACTS

- Statistically, most children who are overly fat at age nine have gained the extra weight between the ages of six and nine.
- The average yearly weight gain during these school years is seven pounds—that is, about nine ounces a month.
- Most moderately active children this age need about 2,000 calories a day, but the range is quite large, depending on body build, activity, and inherited metabolism.
- Children who gain normally do not make new fat cells during this age span. But if they gain too much weight as fat, they do make new fat cells, and these are present for life. This makes losing weight difficult.
- Children who are overweight during the school years tend to grow faster in height and to reach puberty sooner.
- The hormones of puberty in boys tend to turn calories into muscle but in girls tend to turn calories into fat. The girl who is overweight at the start of puberty is not likely to slim down but on the contrary is likely to gain more weight.
- Once a girl starts having menstrual periods, her height growth usually slows down and soon ceases. The average age for starting menstrual periods is twelve and a half. If she is overweight at that time, this can be changed only by losing weight—a feat made difficult by the extra numbers of fat cells.
- From five to puberty, it usually takes about a year of gaining no weight to grow into every 20 percent of extra fat weight.
- Left to their own devices, most children this age eat 35 percent of their daily intake as snacks.
- Only 36 percent of public schools offer daily physical education.

Careers Day!

Here I come to make the rounds from kindergarten through sixth grade, talking about what a pediatrician does.

The kindergarteners, to adults, want to complain about shots. Some have brought along Pediatrician Barbie for my opinion. ("I don't think she's a very good pediatrician," I say haughtily. "She doesn't have a little furry animal on her stethoscope, and she wears a white coat. That might scare the children." Heads nod soberly.)

First through fourth grades want to talk about weird, scary, and disgusting theories of the body: Does eating snot make you sick, and if not, why not? Is it true that when you hiccup you're dead for a second? Do scars ever come open? (This, in a very quiet voice, from a pale young person I just happen to know has recently had an appendectomy.)

Fifth and sixth grades want to talk about highly technical procedures viewed on "Rescue 911" and "ER" and about AIDS, including condoms. They ask, have I ever saved a life or seen a dead person? (Just like that, as one question.) How many years of school does it take to be a doctor, so how old was I when I finished? The answer stuns them. How much money do I make? This answer does not. They end up with an intimidating grand rounds on obscure conditions ("I think he had Wortle's syndrome in his gall bladder," says a serious young man) of relatives and acquaintances.

As I work my way up the grades, I am treated to a tour of the most important issues for children from five through puberty.

For instance, they all passionately want to be in control of their bodies and resent any infringement in this area.

In kindergarten, this passion is mainly expressed as resentment about being "poked." They can understand about the need for shots, but they still regard them as a personal attack. From first through fourth grade I have the feeling that the children think adults have information that we are withholding. Their questions are aimed at unmasking me. In fifth and sixth grades, they are like soldiers in training, ready to take on a threatening world.

Also, I'm reminded how aware they become of Boyness and Girlness, and how intensely they want to fit in. They watch one another like hawks. They have mysterious, specific, important rules for how boys amd girls are "supposed" to behave.

This preoccupation with acceptance is very subtle in kindergarten. The children don't seem to be very aware of themselves as performers with the rest of the class as audience. The class doesn't stop talking to listen to questions or answers. It is like talking to a Greek chorus with a radio playing in the background. Yet even in here, most of the girls are sitting up in front on the rug together, and most of the boys are sprawled on the floor in back.

In first through fourth grades, boys sit in clumps and girls sit in clumps. The boys vie for attention: "Doc! Doc!" they yell, bouncing wildly; three second-graders actually fall out of their seats and without missing a beat hop back up and resume bouncing. The girls aren't quite so aggressive, though they call out too. But in different styles.

"What makes a fart?" asks a boy. Whereas, a girl says: "My mom says that my stepdad farts so much because he drinks too much beer, but she drinks as much as he does but she doesn't fart, she just belches, but she says that he drinks trashy beer, but the beer she likes is good beer, but one day she drank some of his beer but she didn't fart."

The girls ask questions to communicate a story and, it feels like, to establish a relationship; the boys ask questions to get information.

They also comment on one anothers' utterances, which the kindergarteners never do. "That's so dumb!" "She can't ask that, it's against the law!" The boys stage dramatic faints and kick their legs when a girl asks a question, and the girls giggle and shriek when a boy does.

In fifth and sixth grades, the boys have pretty much taken over. The class looks like a wild Chagall sketch, with the boys all levitating sideways toward the ceiling: They are out of their seats, hands raised to the heavens, sputtering out their questions before being called on, and the loudest one with the scariest question wins.

I finally catch my breath enough to call on a girl who has patiently had her hand raised for about seven minutes. "Um," she says, as if recalled from a distant place, "I forget." Both boys and girls look at her approvingly.

Finally, I am forcibly reminded that when children are in groups, the opinion of the group can matter more than the opinion of the adult. This can be hard on the adult.

Except with the kindergarteners, I feel vulnerable. Yes, the kids are vying for my attention, but it is the reaction of their classmates that make that attention desirable—not anything about me. If suddenly that mysterious, ethereal entity called the Mood of the Class decided that my attention was not valuable, I have no doubt that there would be no hands waving in the air.

As they grow, kids increasingly define themselves as Not Adults. This means that sometimes they can and do deny their own close bond to their loving adults in favor of their allegiance to the opinion of the group.

They expect adults to understand that what a kid does because of the presence of the group has really nothing to do with how that kid really feels.

Suddenly I have a memory. Sara and friend, at eleven, swimming in a kid-filled pool. Friend's mother approaches and, following her habit of many years, whistles piercingly through her teeth: "Yoo-hoo, Chickadees!" she yells, waving her bright yellow hat.

"We just went under water," Sara says later, bitterly, "and hoped we'd drown before anybody figured out she meant us."

This, about someone she thinks of and treats at home as her "Other Mother."

One of the mothers in my practice calls the years from nine on "The Land of the Rolling Eyeballs." Yes.

WHAT HELPS

IN GENERAL

- It's still the same old story: Adults decide what, when, and where the family eats; the kid decides how much.
- Away from home, the kid decides everything. The only way to help the kid who is over the "just right" weight range is to educate, trust, and support those decisions. This can be tricky.
- Supporting a decision you think is good means being specific in praise and not focusing on chubbiness. For example: "I admired how you ate the white skin on the orange. I read that's where you get most of the vitamin C. The magazine said you could tell a sophisticated hostess because she left the skin on" instead of, "I'm so proud you ate an orange instead of a Ding Dong. That's fifty calories instead of three hundred zillion."
- Assume that your kid exercises only in your presence and with your knowledge. Counting on physical education classes or trips to the park or even organized sports to provide exercise is unwarranted.

WITH PLANNING MEALS

- The more a kid can participate, the better. The more independent that participation is, the better. The more honest praise from the family about that participation, the better.
- Focusing on calories and deprivation will surely backfire. Focusing on fitting vitamins and minerals and fiber into the available budget is a happier place to start. Kids are very canny consumers when appealed to in this way.
- When the issue of limiting fat in foods comes up, it is both honest and appropriate to give as the reason the health of the adults. Beware, however, not to turn your kid into a worrier—someone who thinks that a little bit of butter is going to give Dad a heart attack.
- When you buy snack food, be unembarrassed about making healthful choices. When asked to purchase Ding Dongs and Cheese Blowouts or whatever, discuss issues such as overin-

flated pricing, additives, FDA supervision of the industry, and concerns about purity (this can get fairly disgusting).

WITH EATING

- Being strict about manners but open about topics of discussion becomes more and more rewarding as you move toward adolescence.
- Conversations that don't focus on weight, calories, good and bad foods, or the faults and foibles of family members are much stronger enforcers of healthful eating than those that do. It's a good idea to come to the table with a topic of conversation handy on the tip of your tongue. If you're stuck, here's a list in order of ascending Kid age: dinosaurs, lowering the voting age to whatever the age the kid is, what profession the newest Barbie doll should be, who should be sent on the next moon landing and why, and why kids today are so much smarter than parents were at the same age.

THE GOAL

Five is halfway to puberty. By puberty, we want our kids to think well of themselves and to have a healthy relationship with us, their parents. If both those things are in place, adolescence has a good chance of being not merely survivable but rewarding, even fun. Handling chubbiness mustn't endanger these goals.

THE CHALLENGE

Clearly, we have reached a very dicey age when it comes to chubbiness. We want a kid to feel good about his or her body. Surely that means that we ought to encourage a kid to be in the "just right" range of weight for height. But if we focus on the chubbiness in an inappropriate way, we can make these crucial years difficult and set the stage for an even more difficult adolescence. Such an inappropriate approach can butt into the three big areas that kids are all about.

• When your parents can't take your shape and your eating patterns and activities for granted, when they act angry or worried or guilty about how you look, it feels as if they are trying to control your body in the most intimate way.

• When your parents focus this way on your chubbiness, it makes you feel as if they are shining a bright light on you as an individual—a light that makes you feel self-conscious and awkward and that gives you stage fright in the group.

• Then you, the kid, may feel as if you have to wrest control of your body from your powerful parents by eating defiantly and refusing to engage in physical activities. That defiance may spread to other areas of life. Or you may hand control over to your parents but resent doing so. That resentment may make you refuse to take any kind of responsibility at all, for anything.

And you may try to escape the "spotlight" effect and feel part of the group in ways that aren't good for you—by being the clown, the bully, the flatterer, the risk taker. You may even try to buy group approval, and brag and lie, or steal things to give or show off.

Finally, you may begin to see your parents—not despite of, but because of, their fond concern—as your adversaries. You may start to confuse your behavior toward adults when you're with your group with how you feel toward your parents in your own heart.

So parents who are worried about chubbiness really need to tackle two things: the chubbiness itself, and the worry. You can't make a worry just go away. You need a plan to deal with it. Otherwise, it can take on a life of its own, making you say and do things that you know make things worse but that you simply can't help.

THE ASSESSMENT

During the years from five until the growth spurt of puberty, the average "just right" child grows about two and one-half inches and gains about seven pounds a year.

But this is average. The range is large.

Just eyeballing a child this age won't always tell you whether that child is at risk for being, or is, overly chubby. Sometimes it can. But so much depends on age and gender and on whose eyeball it is: that of the experienced and dispassionate (I hope) pediatrician, or that of the worried parent, or of the doting grandparent.

One key to eyeballing is to get used to looking at your child in a group of typical children of the same age, all wearing as little clothing as possible. If you are always seeing your kid one-to-one, or with your kid's closest couple of friends, or in a group in which everybody is wearing forty layers of clothing, you could be misled.

Moreover, even the most educated eye can sometimes have trouble determining whether a school-age child is thin, "just right," a little plump, or too chubby. Some children will have bigger frames; their growth in bones will make them gain more weight. Some will add considerable muscular weight, though this variation is much less extreme before puberty than after.

Indeed, the big fooler is puberty. A few kids encounter puberty as early as eight for girls and nine for boys. Puberty brings with it a spurt in both height and weight. Kids in early puberty very often look chubby but are in reality "just right." The problem is, they don't come up to you and say, "Hey, Mom, Dad, I'm starting puberty."

In fact, they may actively conceal that fact, whether from worry or from a zest for privacy. (I can't tell you how many fourteen-year-old girls I've seen because their mothers believe they haven't yet started to menstruate, and who turn out to have been having regular periods since the age of twelve.)

In any case, starting in about fourth grade, a kid may look too chubby either because that is truly the situation or because puberty has begun.

To complicate things further, many school-age children are naturally and normally somewhat padded. That padding keeps them warm in winter, protected when they land backside first, and courageous when tackled by a larger kid. It makes them feel bigger and more powerful. These kids have weight that falls between the 75th and the 90th percentile for height. If they stay in the same percentile over time, they are usually "just right."

A child who is being teased or nagged about extra weight always needs a pediatric evaluation. Sometimes the child is truly extra chubby and needs "lifestyle adjustment." Sometimes the child is truly "just right," and it is the teaser or nagger who needs to be adjusted. And *always* the child needs help in countering the teasing, and ways created to feel self-confident and brave and good about his or her body.

It's also of concern if your "padded" kid thinks he or she is fat and worries about it. A kid who isn't happy in his or her body needs help.

For any concerns about extra fat and extra weight, a visit to the pediatrician for both reassurance and guidance is indicated.

- Is the extra weight due to muscle or fat?
- If it is fat, is it due to "lifestyle" reasons or could it be secondary to some other problem, such as low thyroid hormone? (This is very unusual and especially unlikely if a kid is tall. Hormonal problems almost always slow down height growth dramatically.)
- Is there any medical problem stemming from the extra weight? This too is very unusual, but it's a good idea to check blood pressure in a kid with extra weight.
- Is there any medical or emotional condition that might be contributing to the lifestyle that encourages the extra weight? A kid with huge adenoids and mouth breathing may not be able to smell food. Because so much of taste is really smell, such a kid may be deprived of the pleasure of tasting and depend on bulk for satisfaction. A kid with subtle muscle weakness, coordination problems, or untreated asthma may not be able to exercise as well as friends and classmates. A kid anxious about parental fighting or grades at school may be eating for comfort.
- Is this a change from the previous growth patterns of this kid? If so, what changed? What can we do to reverse the trend?
- Is there so much extra weight, or is it causing so much distress, that the family needs extra services—those, say, of a nutritionist or psychotherapist?
- If there is a decision to intervene, what is it reasonable to expect? Weight *loss* is almost never recommended; if it is, consultation with a nutritionist is vital. But what if the plan is to merely slow the rate of weight gain? How long will it take for your kid to "grow into" the weight that he or she has now?

Once you have determined that your kid is overly chubby but otherwise healthy and that your pediatrician feels that slowing down weight gain by changing lifestyle is the best approach, you can make a plan.

Assessing Fives and Sixes

During the preschool years, the children who are of average weight for height don't look skinny. Their tummies stick out a bit, and their knees and elbows aren't bony. The "just right" kids look, indeed, "just right."

But starting at around five and a half to six, the "just right" kids start to look really skinny.

There's no tummy sticking out. Instead, elbows and knees protrude. This is alarming, because children this age are very bouncy, always bumping around and falling down: You'd think they'd clatter, because they look all bones.

Moreover, children whose weight is a little below average for height but still in the "just right" range—say, at the 30th percentile—will look *really* skinny, with ribs and backbone quite evident.

So the the "just right" kids can look scary. Then, the slightly chubby fives and sixes can look "just right," and the much-too-chubby ones look cute. Only the ones who are much, much too chubby look alarmingly padded.

A Five or Six who is chubby has time to grow into the extra baby fat by slowing down weight gain. For instance, when my friend Manny was six, his weight was just over the 95th percentile for his height. Over the next three years, his weight gain dropped to only three pounds a year. By the time he was nine, he was back on track.

Like many little boys, Manny started gaining that extra baby fat at age four. How come? In Manny's case, it was because he was the youngest of three siblings. His brothers and sisters are *very* active and all too young to drive. Manny spent most of his time after school and on weekends in the car, enjoying the carpool ambience and snacking on whatever the older children had. He was such good company, and so cute and happy, that his extra baby fat didn't seem to be a problem.

Once it became an object of attention, Manny's parents enrolled him in soccer and T-ball. They dropped him at friends' houses instead of taking him along to watch his siblings' games.

Manny was *not* happy with these arrangements. He had loved his previous lifestyle. He wasn't good at soccer or T-ball, and his cheerful, outgoing spirits took a nosedive, which didn't help with making friends.

Happily, his parents neither ignored nor caved in to his distress. His mother tutored him in kicking and throwing the ball; his father ran laps with him. They enjoined his older siblings to cheer Manny on, praising every small step. They made a point of having teammates over and of providing treats and fun for them.

It took about three months for Manny to adjust.

Assessing Sevens and Eights

The child whose weight is average for height will still look skinny, with elbows and knees sticking out. The one whose weight is on the slender side for height—but who is still in the "just right" range—will still look very skinny, with ribs and vertebrae showing. The one who is on the filled-out side of the "just right" range will look Just Right.

In contrast to the younger children, at this age the children who are chubby start to stand out.

I think that this is because at this age you can see a difference between children who are heavy primarily because of chubbiness and those who are heavy only, or primarily, because of body build and muscle development.

For instance, here are three children whose weight is in the 90th percentile for their height. All three are in bathing suits.

The first, who is heavily into gymnastics, is truly muscular. You can see the outlines of the muscles—"not an ounce of fat." The 90th percentile clearly reflects pure muscle.

The second, who loves soccer (but mostly plays defense and doesn't chase around the field much) has a shape that doesn't bulge out much: It is a shape that just casts a larger shadow all over. This child has no double chin. This child moves fast and comfortably, without any fat that jiggles or dimples. There's a roll around the waist if the pants are too tight, and extra chub around the chest, but not anything resembling breasts. This child probably is "just right."

The third child, who has hardly any opportunity or incentive to run around and sweat, has a tummy that sticks out and an extra chin. This child has thighs that rub together and extra chub that dimples and jiggles.

When a kid is overly chubby between six and eight, growing into the extra baby fat has some time pressure attached, especially for girls. Take our friend Cassie. She's the child I worried about in the introduction.

Cassie's Growth Charts

Cassie has always been tall, in the 75th percentile of height for age. If you lined up Cassie with 100 little girls her age, 75 would be shorter and 25 would be taller.

She has also always been heavier than average. Her weight for height used to be in the 75th percentile—that is, if you lined up Cassie with 100 little girls the same height, 75 would weigh less than Cassie and 25 would weigh more. This was true up until age six.

But then, from age six to age seven, Cassie changed her lifestyle. She is now forty-nine inches tall and weighs sixty-six pounds. Her weight for height is off the chart. If you lined up Cassie with 100 little girls the same height, none of them would weigh more than Cassie. The average little girl that height would weigh fifty-one pounds. A little girl at the top of the "just right" range—the 75th percentile—would weigh fifty-six pounds. That's what Cassie would have weighed if she hadn't changed lifestyles.

Up until this past year, in other words, Cassie had been gaining about six pounds a year. This last year, she gained fourteen pounds. Because that was only a bit over a pound a month, it seemed very gradual to her parents.

Growing into the Extra Baby Fat

Cassie now weighs sixty-six pounds. How long will it take her to "grow into" her extra baby fat if she gains only five pounds a year?

If she gains five pounds this year, at age eight she will weigh seventy-one pounds. How tall will she be? We look at the Height for Age chart. Because she is growing in height along the 75th percentile, follow that percentile to age eight and then find the height at that age on the scale below. At age eight she will be about fifty-one inches tall.

Now we turn to the Weight for Height chart. We find fifty-one inches on the scale along the bottom and seventy-one pounds on the weight scale along the sides. Then we see where lines drawn from these two points intersect: It is at the 95th percentile. Cassie is back "on the chart." She is making progress.

If she gains five pounds again the next year, at age nine she will weigh seventy-six pounds. Her height at age nine (following the same procedure as before) will be about fifty-four inches.

We turn again to the Weight for Height chart and see where fifty-four inches and seventy-six pounds intersect. Hurray! We are back on the 75th percentile.

In Cassie's case, it's not too hard to figure out where the extra weight is coming from. New neighbors! Six-year-old girl twins with—hold onto your hat—thirty-eight Barbie dolls! Delicious afternoons of cookies and milk and sorting through piles of clothes and accessories!

Did we cancel the afternoons? Of course not. But Cassie's mother spoke with the mother of the twins, and they changed the snack to nonfat milk and a piece of fruit. Cassie's dad enlisted her in running along as he rode his bike around the block before dinner. And Cassie's mom found a teenager to walk Cassie to school in the mornings instead of driving her. Cassie and the twins joined a dance class, and both sets of parents encouraged practice and home performances. When weather permitted, weekends were filled with outdoor exercise.

Cassie's parents added exercise and made an easy, nearly invisible dietary change. They didn't worry Cassidy with their fears, or nag, or coax, or look at her with That Look when she asked for another helping of macaroni and cheese. They identified what was easy to change. Now together we will monitor Cassie, bringing her in every three months for a "growing check."

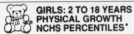

GIRLS: 2 TO 18 YEARS
PHYSICAL GROWTH
NCHS PERCENTILES*

Name **CASSIE**   Record # _____

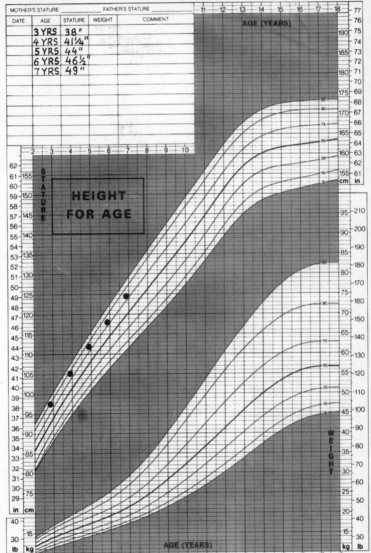

MOTHER'S STATURE _____ FATHER'S STATURE _____

DATE	AGE	STATURE	WEIGHT	COMMENT
	3 YRS	38"		
	4 YRS	41¼"		
	5 YRS	44"		
	6 YRS	46½"		
	7 YRS	49"		

AGE (YEARS)

HEIGHT FOR AGE

STATURE

WEIGHT

AGE (YEARS)

*Adapted from: Hamill PVV, Drizd TA, Johnson CL, Reed RB,
Roche AF, Moore WM. Physical growth: National Center for Health
Statistics percentiles. AM J CLIN NUTR 32:607-629, 1979. Data
from the National Center for Health Statistics (NCHS), Hyattsville,
Maryland.

© 1982 Ross Products Division, Abbott Laboratories

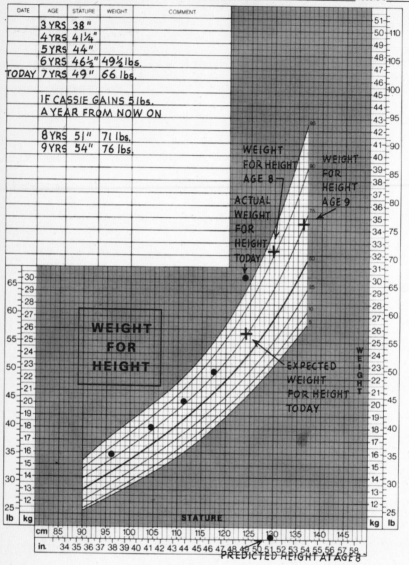

GIRLS: PREPUBESCENT
PHYSICAL GROWTH
NCHS PERCENTILES*

Name **CASSIE**

Record #

DATE	AGE	STATURE	WEIGHT	COMMENT
	3 YRS	38"		
	4 YRS	41¼"		
	5 YRS	44"		
	6 YRS	46½"	49½ lbs.	
TODAY	7 YRS	49"	66 lbs.	
	IF CASSIE GAINS 5 lbs.			
	A YEAR FROM NOW ON			
	8 YRS	51"	71 lbs.	
	9 YRS	54"	76 lbs.	

WEIGHT FOR HEIGHT AGE 8

WEIGHT FOR HEIGHT AGE 9

ACTUAL WEIGHT FOR HEIGHT TODAY

WEIGHT FOR HEIGHT

EXPECTED WEIGHT FOR HEIGHT TODAY

STATURE

PREDICTED HEIGHT AT AGE 8

51214 09893WB
(0.05)/JUNE 1994

LITHO IN USA

If she doesn't slow her weight gain in the next three months, we'll make some more changes.

Finally, if your Seven or Eight shows signs of puberty, a visit to the pediatrician is in order.

A few girls will begin normal changes of puberty at Eight. Most often puberty starts as a tingly, sensitive lump under one nipple, followed in a few months by a few coarse pubic hairs and a lump under the second nipple. Eight is the earliest such changes are normal; below Eight, it is important to make sure that they aren't due to malfunction of ovaries or of thyroid, adrenal, or pituitary glands. Even if the very early puberty is normal, there may be good social and psychological reasons to try to slow things down. So below Eight, a visit to the pediatrician is mandatory if signs of puberty appear.

If puberty begins *at* Eight, such a visit is still a good idea. Even though the onset of puberty is perfectly normal for a particular little girl, she and her parents usually benefit from help in coping with her being so much ahead of her peers.

In boys, normal puberty almost never begins before age Nine. Changes before Nine can mean malfunctions of the pituitary, thyroid, or adrenal glands, and once again a visit to the pediatrician is vital.

Since both girls and boys are very modest at these ages, however, parents may not have a clue that signs of puberty have appeared. For this reason, it's best to continue the yearly routine of a complete checkup at the pediatrician's.

One last note. A very chubby boy may have extra chest fat that he's awfully self-conscious about; other boys may tease him about having "boobs." Parents need to know two things here. First, such a boy should have permission to keep his shirt on during all sports and swimming. Second, very rarely a boy actually will have some breast tissue present. This is never normal. To determine if this could be the case, and to discover the hormonal cause, a visit to the pediatrician is necessary. Don't just assume that the extra tissue is fat. Also, don't be falsely reassured by the very true statement that many boys have a little extra breast tissue during puberty, and that this is normal. Yes, that is the case, but it happens midway during puberty—not beforehand.

Assessing Eights and Up

There is really no "typical" eight- to twelve-year-old. Boys are very different from girls. Some Eights and older are very muscular; others aren't. Some are heading right into puberty; others are only halfway there.

GIRLS

Muscles

Some prepubertal girls are much, much more muscular than others. Genes may make some difference, but the kind of and amount of exercise starts to make even more.

The range of muscular development now is enormous. After all, there are kids in this age range who are exclusively athletes and there are kids who are exclusively computer whizzes.

There are kids who get exercise because their lives demand it (Terry, who works like an adult on the family farm, and Betsy, who rides her bike to school and back, cleans the house because her single father works two jobs, and spends the weekends babysitting four-year-old twins). And there are kids who get exercise because their lives encourage it (Alana, who is not very athletic but whose parents and older siblings play every sport known to humans).

There are kids who get *no* exercise because their lives forbid it (Jackie, who is a latchkey kid whose neighborhood is dangerous and who spends a lot of time watching TV and snacking). And there are kids who get none because their lives discourage it (Francine, whose parents are afraid she'll get hurt or be undesirably "influenced by other children" if she plays actively).

Puberty

It happens sooner than you expect, no matter when it happens.

What is the "right shape" for a Kid entering puberty? Boy, is that a complicated question. First, Kids are so private that they often don't inform parents that puberty has begun. (Though I remember a young man of my acquaintance, age eleven, who put in an urgent phone call to me: "Dr. Nathanson, hair has started to grow on my toes!") Second, kids of both sexes in early puberty often gain a bit of weight, but if they have never been overly chubby before this usually is perfectly normal. Finally, puberty affects girls and boys in dramatically different fashion. Parents may find *You and Your Adolescent* by Leo Steinberg (HarperCollins, 1991) a helpful resource.

However, once puberty has started, parents will find it pointless to assess whether or not their child is too chubby. First, the child will do everything possible to disguise the fact, and will refuse to discuss the subject. Second, hormones have their own life, and trying to intervene while they have sway is pointless. Third, when puberty begins, chubbiness must drop to the very bottom of a parent's priority list—even though it may have risen to the top of the child's own similar list.

Here is what the parents of chubby-prone children need to know about puberty.

GIRLS

If a girl is overly chubby at the beginning of puberty, the hormones of puberty are going to add to the chubbiness. It is extremely rare for a truly chubby girl going into puberty to slim down during the process.

Most girls start puberty at around age ten, and 95 percent have shown signs of puberty—and about half have started menstruating–by age twelve and a half. The first sign of puberty is usually a tingly sensitive lump under one nipple. (If girls aren't warned, they often think this is breast cancer.) Weeks later the other nipple sprouts a breast bud and a few coarse pubic hairs begin to grow. The Girl begins to grow rapidly in height. She also begins to gain more weight, and the rate of weight gain speeds up right after the height gain begins to slow down.

Once a girl starts menstruating, height rate usually slows dramatically and then stops. At this point, of course, a girl can no longer try to "grow into" extra baby fat, but must either learn to make the best of it or endeavor by diet and exercise to lose it.

Parents of chubby prepubertal girls also need to know that most of the time the extra chubbiness produces accelerated height growth and accelerated puberty. That is, a girl who probably would have started puberty at Ten might start puberty at Nine if she is overly chubby for several years beforehand.

But the most important thing for parents of chubby girls entering puberty to remember is that it is futile, fruitless, and cruel to expect their daughters to slim down at this point. Restricting food, "having a chat" about diet and exercise, imploring the pediatrician for prescriptions for appetite suppressants—these cries of anxiety from parents produce only guilt and anger, self-consciousness, and a feeling of helplessness and failure in the young girl.

WHAT IS THE BEST COURSE FOR PARENTS OF GIRLS IN THIS SITUATION?

Find every way you can to help your child feel good about herself.

First and foremost, this means seeking out and listening to her opinions—about everything. Discuss with her many topics having nothing at all to do with her appearance, behavior, and habits of life. Try to keep judgmental comments (criticism and too-fulsome praise) to a minimum.

Second, help her into situations and activities that give her a feeling of accomplishment, autonomy, and independence: learning a new skill, earning money, finding an overriding interest, becoming an academic or artistic or musical achiever, participating in sports in which weight is either an advantage or not a disadvantage, and perhaps most importantly, finding friends who value her self without devaluing her appearance.

Third, protect her from the criticisms, nagging, and even careless comments of other family members.

Fourth, help her to look her best. Often this means attention to skin (no child need have significant acne; get medical help), hair, fingernails, and clothing. But with the greatest of tact.

Fifth, make sure she has the opportunity to know all the facts of puberty. Get for her, and read yourself, a good book on the biology of growing up, like *What's Happening to My Body?* (Book for

Boys; Book for Girls), by Lynda Maderas (New Market Press, 1991). Give her the dignity of privacy, but try to show her that you are open to questions without being shocked or offended.

Finally, ensure that your daughter feels loved—every ounce of her. A child who feels unloved, who suspects she is disappointing her parents and letting down everyone's expectations, is a prime candidate for all kinds of drugs, from tobacco ("it suppresses your appetite") onward. If your family has a religious affiliation, cherish it; religious youth groups have saved the egos of many youngsters of all shapes and sizes.

If and when you and your daughter can talk about her weight, mostly listen. If asked for advice, suggest the program called Shapedown if it is available in your area (see page 193 at the end of this chapter) as a way to keep the inevitable weight gain under some control and to feel at peace with her changing body. And tell the truth: that her chances for *losing* weight will increase greatly when she has finally reached adult height and can embark on a long-term lifestyle change that emphasizes exercise and healthy eating habits. For many girls, that can be as early as the mid-teens.

Be alert to early signs of eating disorders. A restricted or bizarre diet, sudden weight loss, a preoccupation with food, any suspicion of binging and vomiting, the delay or ceasing of menstrual periods indicate a need for early medical attention.

BOYS

Overly chubby boys entering puberty have hormones on their side more than girls do. Testosterone is a muscle-building hormone.

Here's what can help your overly chubby son at this time:

Read everything above, in the Girl's section, about helping a youngster feel autonomous, self-confident, and loved.

Have your pediatrician write a note for school that he is to keep a shirt on during swimming and PE, so that he isn't teased about "having boobs."

Treat puberty with dignity. Talk with him early, no later than Ten, about such topics as wet dreams. (Make sure he knows what to do about the sheets so that he doesn't have to fear each episode.)

Be sure he knows that about 75 percent of boys will develop a bit of breast tissue in mid-puberty, after about age fourteen and that it does not mean either that he has cancer or is turning Female.

Let him dress and wear his hair like his friends, even though you nearly pass out every time you see him. (Gangs are another story, and are way out of the league of this book.)

If possible, help him find work or play or exercise that actively develops muscles. This may be much more acceptable than aerobic exercise; running and sweating makes many chubby young boys feel awkward, and they hate the feeling that the extra weight "jiggles." Lifting weights, carrying heavy loads, digging and carting things around produces gratifying muscle.

Find out as much about adolescence as you can, and about how parents can use their skills and love to help their kids escape the terrible risks of precocious and promiscuous sex, of drugs, and of depression. In fact, most teenagers do not go through such extremes of rebellion and self-destructive behavior. Believe it or not, most parents turn out to be on mutually appreciative terms with their grown-up Kids.

THE PLAN

Helping chubby kids grow into extra weight requires changing patterns of exercise and of eating. This is a long-term commitment, like marriage.

So, like marriage:

- It's a good idea to be sure that all the partners are at least willing, if not enthusiastic; and that they have an idea of what they're getting into.
- Daily habits and rituals need to be so easy to follow that they are automatic—not renegotiated every day.
- Affection and support need to reign. Teasing, sarcasm, nagging, criticism, and use of force aren't helpful.

Parents who really help their chubby kids have one thing in common. They don't feel guilty, and they aren't impatient. This makes it easier to create automatic habits and rituals that foster changes in exercise and eating. It also makes it easy to help the chubby kid feel loved and enjoyed and cute.

Before designing a plan, it's a good idea to confront those issues of guilt and impatience.

WHOSE FAULT IS THE CHUBBINESS?

When a kid is extra-chubby, it's almost always in the context of "following the rules." That is, nobody did anything wrong. Another kid with a different metabolism living exactly the same lifestyle might not be chubby at all.

Extra chubbiness happens over a long period of time. It happens because more calories are taken in on a regular basis than are burned off in growth, activity, and "waste." The extra calories almost always come from a diet that our culture regards as normal and wholesome. And the insufficient activity isn't due to laziness but almost always to normal—even desirable—variations in temperament, interests, and opportunities.

Blaming the child, yourself, your coparent, your job, your day-care person, or whomever is not only self-defeating but also inaccurate. Take that anger outside and walk it off.

As for the problem of parental impatience, considering the following questions will help you get a handle on it.

HOW IMPORTANT IS IT TO HELP A KID GET CONTROL OF THE EXTRA CHUBBINESS?

To answer this, we need to know what kind of difference the chubbiness is making to the kid now and what difference it is likely to make in the future. Is a kid likely to slim down without intervention by adolescence or adulthood? And if not, what are the implications for health and happiness?

We know that if a child is chubby to the point of being obese at age seven, the chance of his or her being obese as an adult is about 40 percent. If a child is obese at age eleven, the risk increases to 75 percent.

So keeping a kid from growing into an obese adult is probably a pretty good reason to intervene early on.

But you're not just thinking ahead to adulthood; you're thinking ahead to adolescence. Very chubby teenagers can get into a great deal of trouble from trying to lose weight. One study showed that 80 percent of teenagers who tried to diet on their own had major physical discomfort, including headaches, constipation, and nervousness; they also had poor concentration for mental tasks. Some of the girls had irregular menstrual periods.

Moreover, the road to anorexia nervosa and bulimia often starts with a self-imposed, unregulated diet.

If unsupervised dieting is a danger, staying extra-chubby as a teenager has its own problems, including discrimination in college admissions, employment, and romance.

Finally, there is some evidence that kids who are extra-chubby may feel distressed about the situation they find themselves in but don't feel bad about *themselves* until adolescence. Then they do.

An adolescent who feels bad about him- or herself is more vulnerable to seeking relief in drugs, sex, and other dangerous behaviors and is less likely to free up energy for academic, artistic, athletic, or other types of achievement.

Even if that weren't the case, it's a sad thing to be a teenager feeling bad about oneself.

How hard is it for a chubby kid to slim down?

There are only two ways to slim down: grow into the weight you already have or lose weight. It is very very hard to *lose* weight. Studies show that 80 to 90 percent of children who *lose* weight return to their previous weight percentiles—that is, to degree of chubbiness.

By definition, kids who have not yet reached puberty have a lot of growing yet to do. That means that they don't have to lose weight but need to grow into the weight they already have. This may not be easy, but it is easier than trying to lose weight.

This means that the earlier in kidhood that you start growing into extra baby fat, the easier it is to do so. As a kid approaches puberty, at eight or older, it becomes trickier and trickier. Your visit to the pediatrician should help you to have perspective on just how many months or, more likely, years it will take.

It will also take commitment to a change in lifestyle for the whole household—not just the chubby kid, and not even just the parents—but also siblings and grandparents and even the dog, who will have to adjust to more walks and a change in the aesthetic quality of the table scraps.

It will also take tolerance of "backsliding." There will be months in which the weight gain is more than desirable, times when you just can't manage the lifestyle changes. It is far more important to rest easy during these times than it is to impose restrictions that make a kid—or the family—miserable.

Once the kid is in the "just right" range, the same lifestyle changes need to be maintained to hold the fort. Happily, by then they should be habitual and pleasant.

WON'T IT BE EASIER TO WAIT A FEW YEARS AND SEE IF THE PROBLEM SOLVES ITSELF?

I wouldn't advise this. Not in today's world. Today, the forces that sponsored the initial extra baby fat are likely to encourage its persistence: an abundance of cleverly advertised high-fat and high-calorie foods; lack of everyday exercise; reduced school budgets with consequent decrease in playground action and physical education classes; seductive TV and video games and computers.

It is true that some chubby kids spontaneously slow down their rate of weight gain and grow into their extra chubbiness before puberty. But we don't know which ones will and which ones won't.

What we *do* know is that chubby kids are likely to reach puberty earlier than they would have if they weren't chubby.

With boys, this may in fact help the chubbiness. The testosterone of puberty helps them to make muscle rather than fat. But with girls, the hormones of puberty inspire more fat collection.

Moreover, with kids of either sex, extra fat seems to encourage the production of more fat cells. Kids of normal weight don't increase the number of fat cells during this age period; chubby kids do. And those new fat cells will be "hungry." This can accelerate the rate of acquiring extra baby fat. Thus a kid who is in the 95th percentile of weight for height in first grade may be well off the chart by third grade.

So my strong vote is not to wait for nature to take her course. You can't count on nature to do what you want.

The most important thing is not to help the chubby kid slim down. It is to foster your kid's ability to take charge of his or her life, make decisions and stick to them, make mistakes and learn from them.

So the most important thing for parents to do for a chubby kid is to fill these years with experiences that make a kid feel successful and in charge. This means mostly focusing on a kid's strengths rather than on a kid's weaknesses. It means not forcing a tone-deaf kid to take piano lessons; not enrolling a klutzy kid in gymnastics or ballet if that makes him miserable. It means bragging about your kid's achievements. It means not comparing your kid to other kids who are slimmer, smarter, more coordinated. It means letting your kid know that you find him or her delightful, cute, and clever. It means laughing at your kid's jokes; or if you can't laugh, fall down moaning dramatically and clutching your stomach.

It means expecting mistakes and addressing them philosophically rather than flying off the handle. Most of all, it means listening to your Kid, really listening, not responding automatically.

And it means getting help if you can't manage this. If you find that your concern about chubbiness makes it hard for you to give your kid freedom, responsibility, and trust, I urge you to obtain some counseling for yourself.

Exercise

For chubby school-age kids, the first and main focus of parents who want to help has to be on exercise. (See the introduction for a discussion of the literature on this topic.)

Why?

- Dieting, in the sense of counting calories and depriving oneself (or being deprived of) desired foods not only doesn't work; it can be dangerous. Dieting makes the whole family focus on a kid's weight. That's not only terrible for the targeted kid; it can take over as the Family Problem. This can allow other problems in the family to go unsolved. The kid can become angry and depressed and cheated and rejected. This can lead to sneaking food, to binging in secret, and eventually to serious disorders like anorexia nervosa.

• Once a kid hits school age, what that kid is offered to eat is mostly out of parents' control. Parents can certainly change the "food atmosphere" at home (see below), and that is desirable and helpful. But it's only a small part of the overall plan.

• The right kind of exercise not only burns calories. It also gives a kid a good feeling about his or her body, skills, and courage. Regular exercise actually changes metabolism, so that the body burns off more extra calories rather than turning them into fat.

• It's addictive. If you exercise consistently for a couple of months, you don't want to go without it.

I can hear some parental moans out there. It is true that some children, and some families, have a true aversion to exercise. I know: My mother regarded exercise with the same distress with which she viewed grammatical errors. The only running she ever did in her life was during college. She had persuaded the physical education department that what she really needed was a nap. But she had to dash from her Latin class to the infirmary to get to her nap on time. I was an adult before I discovered that I really do like to puff and sweat.

But you can design ways for your exercise-resistant kid to sweat and puff. Ways that will make him or her feel good and that can be integrated into the schedules of parents and families. It may not be easy to set up the initial program, but the effort is well worthwhile.

There are several requirements when it comes to getting a kid to exercise in a way that helps him or her grow into extra weight.

First, the exercise should make a kid feel good, not like a klutz.

Many chubby kids don't appreciate activities in which they don't look as good (tutus, bathing suits) or are as coordinated as the other kids in the class.

Second, the exercise should be aerobic. That is, the kid should breathe hard and sweat.

Third, the kid should exercise for half an hour a day, five days a week, minimum. The ideal is one hour a day, seven days a week. That's puffing and sweating the whole time.

There are many different kinds of exercise.

There's the kind you get merely by being an active kind of person.

Jacob, who is nine, plays no sports: He can't stand having somebody win and somebody lose. His school offers daily physical education class, so you'd think he'd get daily required sweaty activity. Not so. Jacob has mastered the art of being on the outskirts of the action. Jacob is mostly to be found in the outfield, on the bench, in the wrong place for a pass. He tells me, in confidence, that he hates the feeling that people are chasing him, or aiming the ball at him, or counting on him to do something with it.

However, Jacob has always regarded the world—including my exam room and, I fear, the waiting room—as a giant personal jungle gym. He can circumnavigate a chair, any chair, without putting a foot on the floor. Jacob never walks. He hops, boogies, twirls; he hurtles over fire hydrants (not recommended from an injury point of view) and twirls around parking meters and finds something to kick and run after.

"Jacob," says his mother, "is the only child I know who comes back from a trip to the library out of breath and sweaty."

The librarians are usually in the same condition after Jacob visits. I know I am.

If your chubby kid, girl or boy, has any of Jacob's tendencies, make the most of them. Take extra time to get places, and avoid driving there. School yourself to be inured to the noise and fuss that goes along with accompanying a Jacob anywhere. Resist the temptation to get him to slow down or stop for a few minutes for a snack. See if your Jacob is interested in a skill-forming, noncompetitive activity such as juggling (as you get good at it, you can use heavier balls; bending over to pick up the dropped ones is excellent exercise), biking, rollerskating, and karate.

Don't make him or her sign up for team sports.

There's the kind of exercise you get in the ordinary course of daily life.

Yvette, at seven, loves school. She is the top reader in her class and draws the best pictures. She adores her teacher and is thrilled when Ms. Rodriguez asks her to do anything at all for her. Yvette is determined to get a perfect attendance record.

"We started off carpooling," her mother says, "but after all, the school is only five blocks away. Of course, she's too little to cross all those busy streets, and the neighborhood isn't 100 percent safe.

"Then I found out that one of her friends lives right next to the school. We get up an hour early, and I walk her to her friend's house, and then that dad walks the two of them to the school when it opens. I pick up Yvette there when I get off work. On the weekends, I take the other little girl, so it works out.

"Usually we just walk fast. Sometimes we go over her spelling words or whatever. I hear more about her life on those walks than I ever heard when we were driving. But three days a week, I manage to 'oversleep' by about five minutes so we really have to run. I don't know about Yvette, but I feel great with the exercise."

Another thing: chores. Setting the table and cleaning up your room aren't aerobic. But here are some jobs that can be: washing the car; shoveling snow; sweeping, raking, digging, or hauling anything; walking or running with a dog; hunting for a cat.

How do you make them aerobic? Well, you could participate aerobically yourself and let your activity be contagious. You could initiate play during the chores: a water fight washing the car, a snowball fight, egging on the cat rather than truly trying to catch her.

What if you are a single parent and are too exhausted from work to help your kid get exercise from the routines of daily life?

Consider the Big Sister and Big Brother organizations, or networking through the Parents Without Partners groups. Your kid needs the security of having other adults who care for him or her, anyhow.

There's the kind of exercise you get from playing with other kids at and after school and on weekends.

There's the school playground before and after school, at recess, at physical education. The park on weekends. There are bikes, roller skates, roller blades, balls, bats, and racquets.

Aren't there?

Not necessarily. First, to take full advantage of all these, kids need two things: skills and companions.

It pays off amazingly to make sure that your kid is comfortable doing what the other kids of the same age and sex are doing. Parents often assume that "every kid" can catch and throw and play on the monkey bars, that kids learn by doing. But this ain't necessarily so.

When you are chubby, it can take a lot of strength and practice to brachiate along the overhead bars, climb a tree or a pole, twirl around the low bar, even pump the swings. Finding a place to practice where your kid won't feel self-conscious and then being an admiring and encouraging coach will earn you a great deal of gratitude. So will playing catch, running along beside the bike, and serving as a stopping post for inline skating.

Second, don't take it for granted that there *is* running around on the playground at school.

Visit. Ask questions.

At many schools, kids don't run around in the playground during recess or lunch: Either they are not allowed to or the customs of their gender or the limitations of their chubbiness don't let them. Only 36 percent of schools have daily physical education classes.

It is a truly sanguine adult who can say, "Most children run around during much of their day, often when their parents do not see them." (*Let Them Eat Cake! The Case Against Controlling What Your Children Eat,* by Kleinman, Jellinek, and Huston, Villard Books, 1994, p. 10.)

If your chubby kid doesn't like running around, it's probable that his or her friends don't either. They may spend most of their time together at the computer, making models, watching TV. Making snacks. Schmoozing.

If your child carpools or buses to and from school, spends all day sitting in class, has an hour or two of homework and another of TV, he or she may not be getting any running around at all.

Once you analyze your kid's activity level, you may find lots of ways to increase exercise. But one warning: Don't try to impose new friends or reject the old ones. Instead, take your kid's buddies along to the park or playground. But make sure that you do so in a way that doesn't make them feel self-conscious or defensive.

There's the kind of exercise you sign up for in groups.

If all goes well, these are great: the fun of playing with friends and learning together can't be beat. But the kid has to be carefully matched with both the activity and with the leader/teacher and group.

Some chubby kids do like soccer, hockey, and other aerobic team sports. But some will pretend to like them because their parents so clearly want them to participate. These kind and willing-to-please kids may spend a lot of time on the bench, or feeling incompetent, or wandering around trying to avoid the action.

So if, like Jacob, your kid is competition-adverse, look into nonsports activities that still can be very active. These include Girl Scouts and Boy Scouts, Boys and Girls Clubs, the YMCA and YWCA.

If at all possible, observe a meeting or class, or at least meet the leading adult, before presenting the idea to the kid. You know your own kid. Is this somebody he or she will like and respect? Are the other kids like yours in personality and interests? Are there other chubby kids in the class? Are the classes or meetings mostly active, adventure-oriented, or devoted to sedentary crafts and projects?

If your kid attends a few meetings and then shows a pronounced dislike, I would be careful about forcing the issue. It may be that he or she really feels like a fish out of water and that each session is painful. That's never been known to help anybody.

There's the kind of exercise you pay to engage in.

If you can afford them, these often are adored by the kid, who frequently comes to them equipped with an already-formed passion.

Be careful, though. Some kinds of "exercise" that one thinks of as vigorous really aren't. Most of them can be modified so that they become aerobic, however. Here are some examples:

- SWIMMING. A very good swimmer doesn't get out of breath. There's no gravity to resist. The cool water may even make one's metabolism go into nonaerobic gear, which tends to make calories go into fat more easily. Modifications: training for swimming by running laps and lifting *light* weights, half an hour for each half hour of swimming.
- DOWNHILL SKIING. You go up in a chair and come down via gravity. Not much in the way of aerobics, unless (like me) you use up a zillion calories in falling ski-tip down into snowbanks and extricating yourself, or in heart-pounding terror. Modifications: Learn cross-country skiing or snowshoeing, or save money by carrying the skis up rather than using the lift. (Yeah, sure!)
- HORSEBACK RIDING. The horse gets the exercise. Modifications: Earn the right to ride by mucking out the stall every time; play "horses" by running and jumping over obstacles so you can see the course from the horse's point of view; spend at least twenty minutes vigorously brushing and grooming your steed.
- GYMNASTICS CLASSES. In many classes, a kid spends a lot of time watching demonstrations and waiting in a line. A chubby kid may also spend a lot of time hiding and avoiding. Modifications: Talk to the teacher about developing a special fitness class for children who need more aerobic exercise and fun rather than competition.
- FITNESS CLASSES. These are great *if* you really do attend regularly and *if* your kid really participates. But I can't tell you how many families I see whose memberships, bought and

paid for, sit idle—as do the kids. For this to work, I'd strongly suggest fitting in a regular time and vowing not to bump this activity for anything: not for errands, or visiting relatives, or inclement weather. Also, I'd urge getting a friend of your kid's to go along, even if you have to help with the funding. Third, I'd ask Kid to teach you some steps and then be a real klutz when it comes to learning them, if possible twisting yourself into a pretzel and falling onto the floor. I'd let your kid hear you telling your friends that thank God he or she inherited a coordination gene that must be recessive in you.

• KARATE. If the class has a charismatic teacher, one who inspires self-confidence and the learning of poise and assertiveness, this may make up for the lack of aerobic qualities in the activity. Such an adult may even get an older kid out running and lifting weights to train for class. But don't be surprised if this doesn't happen.

WHAT ABOUT TURNING OFF THE TV SET?

There have been many studies on the effect of TV watching on chubbiness. It's a pretty confusing picture, believe it or not. Many show a relationship between hours of watching and the degree of overweight, but it's not clear what the reason is. Increased snacking, because of all the "food cues" on programs and ads? Or is it inactivity? (One study showed that watching TV uses up *less* energy than simply resting in bed!) Or is it that chubby children watch more TV because they are already chubby?

No study, however, shows that watching TV is a helpful adjunct to growing into baby fat!

What is the kid going to do instead of watching TV? If you can answer that question, then you have the answer to the first one.

Nutrition

From age Five until the spurt of puberty, Kids often persist in the pattern of "a good breakfast, fair lunch, and just pick at dinner." However, there are variations: Some Kids can't stand breakfast and pick a different meal to eat well.

As Kids grow older, they get increasing amounts of their daily food intake in the form of snacks; by the middle grades, most Kids get about a third of their daily calories in that form.

Kids who are prone to chubbiness and those who are not share both tendencies, plus another important characteristic: They do a great deal of their eating away from home, or at least out of their parents' sight, in their rooms (please don't write and tell me what you've found mummified under the bed) or home alone after school.

Finally, the caloric intake of kids this age varies dramatically from meal to meal, from day to day, and from kid to kid. Inherited metabolism, activity level, rate of growth, and body build all play a role. You could keep a daily log for a week of everything eaten by two different kids of the same age, sex, and weight, and those logs could differ by a thousand calories a day.

For parents of kids prone to chubbiness, all this makes for worry and feelings of helplessness, which tend to come out as trying to control how much, and what, your kid eats in your presence. Unfortunately, most of the time this means making comments, nagging, sighing, making faces, and so on. In reality, the only way to control what your kid eats in your presence is to control what foods you buy and bring home. And even then, you are only controlling a small part of your Kids' total intake of food and drink.

However, this is still mightily worthwhile. Implementing the suggestions below about how to govern eating at home gives Kids this age the feeling that parents know what is good for the family and will enforce that policy. When parents can give Kids this conviction in the intimate realm of food and eating, Kids are likely to believe that parents will hold the line in other areas, too—such as reasonable expectations about responsibility, behavior, and achievements.

The key, however, is a combination of honesty and tact. It is important that controlling what food is bought and the rituals of eating make a statement about the family's health and about not being ripped off by advertisers, rather than a statement about your Kid's weight problem. You can talk about pesticides and animal fats, about fiber and colon cancer, about the nutritional wisdom of eating foods "that remember where they came from" rather than highly processed ones. You can talk about the morality of ad campaigns designed to lure kids into smoking cigarettes, drinking gallons of whole milk and six-packs of soda. You can talk about your childhood candy intake and its relationship to your upcoming root canal, and describe that procedure in detail with sound effects. But if you talk about counting calories, and percentages of fat calories, and keeping portions reasonable, your efforts will backfire.

Kids need to feel in charge of what they eat. They need to choose which food and how much of it to eat at each meal and each snack. Parents can only control the selection offered at home. They can't even totally control that; kids can use earned money or allowances for their own indulgences. But parents of kids prone to chubbiness don't need to fill the cabinets with temptations.

One final word: It is really hard to acquire a nutritional deficiency during this age range. A Kid who eats anything close to an ordinary variety of foods will get all the recommended daily requirements of vitamins and minerals. This is because so many ordinary foods are fortified with vitamins and minerals. The only exceptions might be calcium in a Kid who consumes no dairy products and iron in a Kid who eats no meat, fish, fowl, or green vegetables. If your Kid falls into either category, or if your Kid is set upon a truly restricted diet or a truly bizarre one, consult your pediatrician and consider a consultation with a qualified nutritionist.

Milk

Kids over five—chubby or not—don't need whole milk or low-fat 2% milk. More than half the calories in whole milk are fat, and nearly one-third of the calories in low-fat 2% milk are fat. Because the daily intake of fat should be only one-third the total calories, drinking 16 or more ounces of either kind of milk doesn't leave much for the rest of the daily food intake.

Nonfat or 1% milk or a mixture of half of each is a healthier solution for all kids and can make a dramatic impact on the calorie intake of the chubby ones.

Kids in this age group need about 16 ounces a day up until age eight or so. Then girls should increase the amount, because recent studies have shown that in the years approaching puberty girls use that extra calcium for building bones for life.

Juice

Why does juice seem healthier than other sugary drinks? Most of the time, it's not. Read the label: Most beverage juices like apple juice or grape juice contain less than 2 percent of any vitamin or mineral other than potassium. (It's very hard for a healthy person to have a potassium deficiency.)

The sugar in juice is just as caloric as the sugar in soda.

Moreover, drinking sweet juice can be habit forming. Many kids prefer it to water when they are thirsty and to milk at any time.

Breaking a juice habit takes parental determination plus an explanation that doesn't focus on the chubbiness issue. I suggest that you give as an explanation the lack of nutrition in juice. You might even want to ask your kid how the juice advertisements make you think that juice is good for you, without ever telling you how. Then you can put the whole thing into the context of not being lured by advertisements.

Soda

Sugary sodas contain about 150 calories for each 12 ounces (except for ginger ale, which contains only 113). Because an excess of only 100 calories a day over a year can theoretically produce an extra 10 pounds of weight, cutting out a daily soda can make a real difference to a chubby kid—*if* those extra calories don't just get consumed in a different form.

If your kid is truly "addicted" to soda with caffeine in it, there is a tiny possibility that he or she feels better on caffeine and is seeking it out. Because this can happen to kids with attention deficit disorder, you may wish to ask your kid's teacher and pediatrician about this possibility.

Diet sodas have their own, more subtle problems. Although they have no calories, they do tend to persuade kids to drink when they are not thirsty. Moreover, because they are carbonated, they fill up the stomach. If a kid is used to always having a full stomach, an empty one is going to feel very unnatural, rather than a normal way to feel when it is time to eat. These both can reinforce a chubby kid's dependence on outside, rather than internal, cues about when to eat and drink.

Cola drinks that contain phosphate have been implicated in decreasing bone thickness in girls, though not in boys, after puberty.

Food

Trying to enforce how much a kid eats will backfire. And because at this age most kids serve themselves, the size portions in an "ideal" diet are irrelevant, with one exception. That is, it's a good idea to keep servings of meat, especially of red meat, on the small size—about the size of a playing card from a regular deck. Even lean meat contains significant amounts of fat.

What parents can enforce is how the whole family regards food, and what foods are bought by parents. The key is not to focus on weight gain or chubbiness issues, but on overall healthy habits.

When parents envision changing eating habits, they tell me that they foresee life as a daily battle. And that, of course, won't work. You can't conduct the long-term campaign a chubby kid needs to grow into his or her weight if you are exhausted from daily renegotiations and compromises and disobeyed commands.

HOW JOCELYN TURNS THREE RAW CARROTS AND AN APPLE INTO A DING DONG

SCENE: A THIRD-GRADE LUNCHROOM

Three raw carrots from Jocelyn to Maria in exchange for four Ritz crackers. (Maria likes only Saltines, and she will trade these carrots for Saltines.)

One apple from Jocelyn to Jorge in exchange for two American cheese singles. (Jorge's concept of food groups is: crunchy, chocolate, spicy, and salty. Bland and creamy doesn't do a thing for him.)

Four Ritz crackers and two American cheese singles from Jocelyn to Renee in exchange for a slice of angel food cake with pink frosting and a promise from Jocelyn to be Renee's bus buddy on the field trip tomorrow.

Angel food cake with pink frosting from Jocelyn to Kayla in exchange for a Ding Dong and the right to play with Jocelyn's Gymnast Barbie for the rest of lunch hour.

How Can You Make Changes That Can Become Habits Fast?

First, start with what is easiest.

Often this means changing your kid's beverage. That may mean changing what your kid drinks for thirst, between meals—from juice or soda to water, and changing from whole milk or low-fat 2% milk to nonfat or 1%.

Sometimes it means changing what you pack for school lunch, bearing in mind that after first grade practically nobody eats what they bring; they trade. See box on lunches.

It might mean changing how you cook, from frying to methods that don't use fat. Or doing away with cream sauces and fat-rich cheese toppings.

Second, if you make big changes, do so where they will pay off most.

The one that pays off most is one that is very hard for some families. It is structuring eating, especially in the afternoon and evening and on weekends. This means that meals *and snacks* occur at regular times. It means eliminating handouts—the handful of this, the container of that—munched on and off throughout the day on impulse or from habit, without regard to hunger.

This means that boxes of munchies are simply not brought into the home—at least by parents. Snack foods are always available, however. See the Appendix for suggestions.

Third, be definite about what is your job and what is the kid's job.

The rule that worked well for infants, toddlers, and preschoolers was: "Parents decide what food gets put on the table, and the child decides how much to eat." But what point is there in continuing that rule when your school-age kid is getting so much of his or her food away from home? Isn't it time to start restricting portions and not allowing second helpings?

No. It isn't. Kids need to decide how much they are going to eat of what is there every single time they are presented with food and drink. Parents who try to control that part of eating for them injure a very important part of a kid's soul: It feels to the kid as if he or she isn't trusted in the most basic and intimate way. Not only will the kid rebel, refusing to eat what is there and sneaking other foods, but the kid will also feel uncentered and out of control when it comes to eating.

IT'S IN THE (BROWN) BAG

Lunch at school is not about nutrition; it's about socializing. It's about popularity and power and ego. Trying to control what a kid eats for lunch is pretty much out of parents' hands.

There are two exceptions to this.

First, your kid may tell you that if you pack a really great lunch, that lunch will probably be eaten, not traded. The question is, does a really great lunch mean trouble? If a really great lunch is too difficult or time consuming for a parent or kid to

---

prepare without resentment, is too expensive, or is composed mostly of sugar or fat, it is trouble.

Really great lunches that are composed mostly of fat are, alas, easy to come by. They include the prepacked lunch and snack trays containing crackers, cheese, cold cuts, and often a dessert. These have enormous amounts of fat. Read the label. A homemade lunch that resembles these has the same problem. A salami and cheese sandwich, corn chips, and cookies, for example adds up as follows:

> Six slices of salami: 426 calories, 307 of them fat
> Two slices of rye bread: 126 calories, practically no fat
> 10 corn chips: 97 calories, 93 of them fat
> 1 tablespoon mayonnaise: 57 calories, 45 of them fat
> 2 chocolate chip cookies: 94 calories, 36 of them fat

Without a beverage, that is: 800 calories, 481 of them fat.

Because they contain most of what many kids regard as the basic food groups—salty, chewy, crunchy, creamy, and chocolate—they can be quite habit forming, too.

Better to make not-so-great lunches (from a kid's point of view). Even if your kid trades away the whole thing, the resulting trades are not likely to be worse than the prepacked fare. And think of the social skills picked up during lunch hour.

To have the best luck with a tradeable lunch, ask your kid to help. Starting at five, a kid can help pick out things that taste good that are also good for you. A kid can also pick out a treat either to eat or trade. The agreement is that only the treat gets traded for other treats. You can't monitor this agreement, but a kid who feels honored and trusted and who thinks the reason is nutrition and not chubbiness may well keep it pretty consistently.

It also helps to have a kid help prepare lunch. I don't know why; I just know parents tell me this. "I think they bond to it," says Marcie's mom, a Lamaze coach.

Even a Five can spread mustard or peanut butter on bread. Eights can make the whole thing.

SCHOOL-PROVIDED LUNCHES

There are virtues to school-provided lunches. A story in the *New York Times* (October 26, 1994, p. B-1) points out that school lunches as a whole tend to have fewer fat calories than typical home-packed lunches.

Moreover, there is a limited trading value to the school lunch. It is often looked down upon, simply because it is the same for everybody.

ETHNIC LUNCHES

Many ethnic lunches, such as sushi, are lower in fat and calories than the usual school cafeteria or brown-bag fare.

But the same *New York Times* story says that "regardless of gender, race, region, or socioeconomic class, most children in the country seem to eat the same things for lunch. . . .[A principal says that] when new students from immigrant families first attend her school, they often bring lunches from ethnic backgrounds. . . . but after a few months, those same children would be eating cheese or bologna sandwiches or pizza from the hot lunch menu."

As I said, school lunch is not about nutrition.

But it is true that when kids get to school age, this plain old rule will no longer suffice. Instead, parents need a philosophy. I offer the following:

- Food bought for the family is healthy.
- Food is never bought for, served, or prepared differently for the chubby kid from the way it is for the whole family. Reasons for changing patterns of food choice are always those of health, not those of weight reduction.
- Mealtimes are pleasant.
- No expression of nagging, sarcasm, or teasing, no matter how subtle, is tolerated. This includes comments by parents! Especially, it includes no teasing or nagging or coaxing

of the chubby child. Also not allowed is any expression of disrespect to the food or the preparer thereof.

Yes, I realize that living up to such a philosophy may seem as impossible as traveling around the world without ever losing your luggage. And, like that enterprise, this one needs a lot of luck, as well as planning, patience, and interpersonal skills.

But try taking it apart, and the individual steps may seem more manageable:

Food bought for the family is healthful.

Parents really are gatekeepers for what food is bought for the household (as opposed to that bought by kids for themselves).

Moreover, most kids from six up, and most parents, do know what foods are more nutritious than others.

But knowing what's good for you and buying it and eating it are poles apart.

The most common excuse I hear from parents is this: Other family members are used to, fond of, and don't seem to suffer from, high-calorie and high-fat foods and snacks. "It's not fair to Jamie that I don't serve pie for dessert. He asks why he has to go without just because Lee has a weight problem. He says it's not fair. And I guess he's right." Hmm.

I truly believe this is not a food problem; this is a parental authority problem. What is really happening here is *not* that the other kids or adults are deprived of foods they want. They are perfectly free to earn and spend money on such foods for themselves, if they wish.

When parents find this problem occurring and feel as if they are "punishing" other family members in their quest to "help" the chubby kid, I believe that they are really angry at that chubby kid themselves. If you find yourself feeling this way, I strongly suggest that you talk over the situation with your pediatrician or ask for a recommendation to a counselor who can help you come to terms with your feelings.

Let us suppose, though, that you do not feel in any danger of having this happen but that you do feel, as a parent and as a family, deprived of foods that you are used to, fond of, and know are not good—in quantity, on a regular basis—for any of you. Here are some ways to change how your family eats and make it work.

Serve "real dessert" less frequently.

First, I suggest that you tackle that "in quantity, on a regular basis" clause. Instead of having a "real dessert" every night, try cutting down to once a week. And then make it a real dessert indeed, a favorite, and set no limits on how much anybody has or make any requirements about eating vegetables first. Also, no remarks about having "earned" it because of being "deprived" the rest of the week or about "making up for it" by cutting calories the next day. You may feel that way, and it may take weeks to stop feeling that way, but just don't *talk* about it. Talking about it only reinforces those feelings.

Make step-by-step changes in how you shop and cook.

First, completely elminate from the family shopping list only those foods that announce on the label that they contain no (or almost no) nutrients other than fat and sugar: for example, doughnuts, candy bars, potato chips and other crunchies, sodas, most juices. Next, move to a different mode of cooking meat, one that does not involve frying. At the same time, introduce very gradually new foods or foods prepared a different way.

Don't try to change basic patterns of how you prepare and eat meals. Just try to change the content.

If you are a family that doesn't cook but rather thaws and microwaves or brings home takeout, don't suddenly decide that you are going to be a low-cal gourmet chef. Instead, stick to the same guidelines above. Just buy differently. Check the labels for foods that have fewer than 30 percent of the calories as fats. Go in for variety in textures, spiciness, chewing satisfaction, and delicious aromas rather than fats and sugars. Garlic is your friend.

Do involve all the kids in planning, shopping, and serving, but make it fun.

One way, if finances allow, is to put each kid of seven or older in charge of planning, shopping for, and helping to prepare one meal a month. The rule is that the kid must choose healthful foods (make a list) and keep within a certain amount of money. The kicker is: The kid can keep whatever money is left over from that amount. You will be amazed at what foods a kid will buy and eat with this incentive. As a terrific by-product, this completely removes the chubby kid from the role of scapegoat. The scapegoat, if any, is the kid who was in charge of dinner.

This is an excellent way for a kid to feel good about a job well done, to have one-to-one time with a parent, and to learn about the arts and the errors of cooking a meal. It's also a great opportunity for a parent to have fun with the kid. Preparing a meal is an important task and can also be hilarious. If you have enough loud fun at it, the whole family may join in.

Make sure that there is one dish at each meal that you know is liked.

At first, that one dish might be heavily into fat or sugar or both—french fries, creamed corn. As you gradually change how you cook, one hopes that more dishes, ones that are more healthful, will come to be appreciated, and you can phase out the high-fat, low-nutrition ones a bit and still have a favorite at each meal.

Food is never bought, served, or prepared differently for the chubby kid from the way it is for the whole family. Reasons for changing patterns of food choice are always those of health, not those of weight reduction.

Even though the whole family may know, or strongly suspect, that chubbiness is at the bottom of the change in menu, do not suggest by word, look, or tone of voice that this is the case. Once you do, family meals will become painful.

Say, "We need to eat in a healthful way." Stick to that one statement, repeated as often as possible. Discuss what that means, and how it is compatible with delicious eating.

Mealtimes should be pleasant, wherever they are eaten.

Yes, I know that for most families meals are not usually sit-down-together occasions. I don't think that sitting down together is the point; it's talking together in ways that make people feel good.

Suddenly bringing everybody to the dinner table and enforcing

regular camp. Such a camp can be a wonderful or an embittering experience. For a chubby kid to enjoy regular camp:

- There must be no pressure on the kid or the camp to produce any "slimming down." Camp is seen as a fun experience with the learning of skills and making of friends the high priority.
- The kid should already be good at some of the activities offered, both athletics and crafts. Really, really good, if possible.
- If there is an activity that the kid can't or really hates to do, it must be purely, purely optional. The chubby kid who fears the water is not going to learn to love it while being made fun of.
- The emphasis must not be on activities requiring very skimpy or body-revealing clothes, such as in a dance camp.
- The kid has a "camp" personality, social and outgoing, and has a track record of being liked.
- Nobody makes any restrictions on diet. Parents and pediatrician do not write special requests on the camp physical form; parents mail "care packages" of cookies just like everybody else's cookies.

Weight-loss programs abound, but many are not geared to kids. One that is, and that works, is the program called Shapedown.

Shapedown is a unique program developed in 1979 at the School of Medicine, University of California, San Francisco with support from federal and health agencies. The program is family oriented, and it is families—not just chubby kids—that change and become healthier during treatment and maintenance. As their pamphlet states,

"SHAPEDOWN builds on the strength of the family. It gently and effectively supports families in creating an active lifestyle and a healthy but not depriving diet. Parents tune up their nurturing skills to curb their child's emotional overeating and sharpen their limit setting skills to prompt their child toward a healthier lifestyle. The child accepts more responsibility for diet and activity and feels happier and safer. Food becomes less imortant, activity more exciting and the child's weight begins to normalize."

It is one of the few programs in which chubby kids who have "slimmed down" don't bounce right back to their previous degree of chubbiness. It is not inexpensive, but if a kid is very, very chubby you may be able to get insurance to cover part of the costs. (Alas, most plans do not cover what would be a very wise preventive medicine measure.)

Even if insurance doesn't cover it, it's a great investment.

THE MORAL OF THE STORY

Chubby kids are first and foremost kids—not chubby—and intervening in the chubby trend means respecting that. Helping a chubby kid means to trust him or her to be able to change in lifestyle, so that eventually the kid will grow into the extra weight. The first emphasis is on exercise; the second on healthy eating, never on dieting. But helping with chubbiness needs to be tactful. Guilt and blame are the enemies, not the chubbiness. If your kid stays chubby but believes that he or she is a delicious, cute, clever, funny person who is liked, trusted, and turned to for opinions and witty sayings, your kid will be ready to take on adolescence with aplomb.

Handouts for Grandparents and Day-care Grownups

When there's another loving adult caring for your child, you want that adult to help your youngster make mostly healthy choices about exercise and eating. And you want to communicate that wish in a way that keeps you friends with the other adult.

The following handouts are written to that adult—grandparent, say, or day-care or preschool person. They are written from the child's point of view, in the child's words.

One way to use a handout is to copy it (there's no copyright problem) and show it to the other loving adult. Another way is to use it as a model for a letter that you write yourself. A third way is to use the letter as a guide for what you might say when you talk with your child's other caretaker.

BABIES ONE TO FOUR MONTHS

Grandparents

Dear Grandma and Grandpa,

Thanks to you, I am having a wonderful time being the Center of the Universe.

You make the most wonderful faces and noises in the world, and you know exactly how to burp me and change my diaper. I guess you must have had some previous experience along these lines.

Clearly, you know a lot about feeding, too. I am glad you support my parents in having me nurse or take high-iron formula. Homemade formulas from evaporated milk don't give me the right balance of nutrition: They don't contain essential fats, and their protein is hard to digest, and they have too much salt and not enough iron.

I'm glad, too, that when you feed me you coo and talk to me and hold me. No bottle propping for you! And how clever you are at telling when I've had enough, and how forgiving when I haven't finished the whole bottle.

Many thanks, too, for not seducing me with juice or foods. I am still getting the basics down pat. Breast milk or formula is about all I can handle right now.

I am hoping to gain about an ounce a day for the foreseeable future, which means until I'm six months old. Thank you for thinking that my ounces are the most adorable ounces in the whole wide world.

I like your ounces, too.

Day-care Grownups

Dear "Other Mother,"

I love how you smile at me and play with me and feed me. You have a superior lap to cuddle in and a great shoulder to spit up on.

The way you hold me and feed me are teaching me that the world is a wonderful, loving place, and that I am a very important person.

First, you help me learn to trust my body's signals. If I can do that, then later on I will be able to judge how much and what kind of food I need. I won't have to diet or deprive myself or worry about how much I weigh.

One way you teach me is that you always hold me when you give me my bottle. You don't just prop it and leave me to my own devices. And when you give me the bottle, you let very clever me find the nipple: You don't just plunk it into my mouth. When I'm done, you don't try to top me off as if I were a gas tank in a car, or scold me when I haven't finished the whole thing. You talk to me while I drink my bottle, so I feel very important indeed.

Second, you let me know what it is to be hungry and then eat and be full. I know this seems like a pretty basic concept, but at my age I'm a pretty basic person. So I'm grateful that you keep me on a pretty regular but not rigid schedule. If you gave me that bottle every single time I made a little squeak, I'd never figure out what hunger is. After all, I squeak when I've got a gas bubble, and when I'm making a poop, and when I want to roll over and can't, and when I want to be walked around the room to look at things.

Finally, I am very pleased you haven't corrupted my palate with juice. I am plenty entertained by the slight taste shifts in breast milk and formula. Such a sweet drink as apple juice makes those slight shifts very boring in comparison. I would hate to make your life miserable by screaming for juice all the time.

At my age, I tend to get mixed up: Being fed and being loved are pretty much the same thing to me. Eventually, I'll have to figure out that they aren't. But it's not time for me to do that yet. I have to get them mixed up now in order for me to see the difference later on.

So lucky for me I've got you. I hope you feel the same way about me.

INFANTS FOUR TO TWELVE MONTHS

Grandparents

Dear Grandma and Grandpa,

I love to be with you. You make me smile and gurgle and feel good.

And I love to make you smile, too. When you feed me and play with me, I will do almost anything to see you happy.

Because you mean so much to me, you can help me a lot as I'm learning to feed myself over these months. I need to learn so much: not just how to get my food into my mouth instead of my ears but also how to decide whether I've had enough of something, and whether to try a new food, and what kind of tastes are my favorites.

It helps me when you schedule regular meals. I need to learn what it means to be a little hungry, and to put up with that feeling for a little while, and then to eat until I'm full, and then stop.

I will learn best when you decide what foods to put in front of me and then let me decide how much of each one to eat. If I refuse something, like a green vegetable, please don't force or coax me. That makes me think that eating is about power, and I am likely to put up a giant fuss that makes us both unhappy. On the other hand, don't take my refusal too seriously: Keep offering the lima beans, or whatever, at other meals and I'll probably wind up eating them. Please don't give me juice to drink instead of water or milk. It is so temptingly sweet, I may start to refuse to drink anything else!

It's time for me to learn how to use my fingers and a spoon. Oh, boy, what a mess! But if I don't learn now, I may insist on being fed after I'm much too old, and you'll have to chase me around the house and coax me and we may even get into fights about it. I sure don't want that.

You are the best dining companions a baby could have. You can share my bib any day of the week!

Day-care Grownups

Dear "Other Mother,"

I love how you take care of me. I'm learning new things every day.

One of the things I'm learning is how to decide what to eat and how much to eat.

You can help me by making our meals together fun and by letting me make those decisions. Let me decide when I'm ready for another bite of spinach or sweet potato or pears. Let me decide when I've had enough. I'm likely to eat a little at one meal and a lot at the next, and that's fine. I will learn best if my eating isn't rushed, and if nobody coaxes me to clean my plate. It is lovely for me when you sit with me smiling and talking, admiring how well I am eating, no matter whether I am chowing down or being very selective, whether I am being messy or tidy. Some meals and some days I'll eat a lot; other times, I'll barely nibble. That's okay.

I will do best on three meals a day and not more than two snacks, one in the middle of the morning and one in the middle of the afternoon, at pretty regular times. I may not even eat much at those snacks.

If I don't like a food, for instance a green vegetable, don't give up right away. If you serve it over and over again for maybe ten times, I'll probably come to put up with it and even enjoy it.

But please don't serve me sweet desserts. In my innocence, I still think that plain old peaches and pears and so on are grand treats. And don't confuse my palate with juice as a thirst quencher; let me have water if you think I'm thirsty. If I refuse water it's not because I don't like the taste; it's because I'm not thirsty. (I'll drink juice even when I'm not thirsty, just because it's sweet!)

Thank you for loving me and feeding me so well.

TODDLERS

Grandparents

Dear Grandma and Grandpa,

You are my favorite people, and I love to be with you. You are so much fun and you think I am wonderful and you make me laugh and feel good.

Since you already do so much for me, I feel perfectly fine about asking you to do one more thing: Help me grow into my adorable baby fat!

I have a little extra tummy and chins and chub all around. Right now, it looks good and nobody teases me. But in a couple of years I won't be so happy to be rounder than my friends. If I can just slow down my weight gain for a couple of years, I'll be in great shape for kindergarten.

So please don't bring me rich treats. If you would like to share an apple or some nonfat cheese and crackers with me, that would be nice— but please save the cookies and candy and wonderful desserts for special occasions.

Thank you for caring about me so much!

Day-care Grownups

Dear "Other Mother,"

You make me very happy when I am with you. I trust you with all my problems.

Here is another one. I am getting a little chubby. Right now, that's fine: I think I look very cute. But in a few years, I don't think I'll be so happy about being rounder than everybody else.

Will you help me grow into my baby fat? Here's what will help.

First, get me to run around and breathe hard and get sweaty and dirty, even though I'd rather sit and play with toys.

Second, help me learn to eat when I'm hungry—not when I'm frustrated or bored or anxious. Please give me planned snacks instead of "munchies" of crackers and raisins and cookies to nibble on. A snack in the middle of the morning and middle of the afternoon would be fine. It could be fruit or crackers and low-fat cheese or low-fat yogurt. Oh, and please don't let me drink apple juice (or other juice) or milk all day long, either.

Third, teach me that food is just food, not a reward. I am all too likely to quiet down or pick up my toys or stop making noise when you offer me a cookie. Oh dear. I do love cookies. But they go right to my chub. I think I could learn to behave for a hug or a smile, if it came from you.

Thank you for helping me!

PRESCHOOLERS

Grandparents

Dear Grandma and Grandpa,

I am so happy that you think I am the cutest person in the world. I think I am, too.

Now that I am a preschooler, I am likely to look skinny to you. My little tummy will go away, and chubby thighs will become less squeezable. But it's still the same Cute Me underneath.

Also, I am supposed to be a finicky eater. I'm likely to eat only one good meal a day and the rest of the time just pick. One day or one meal I may eat lots, and the next, practically nothing. My body tells me how much I need to eat, according to how much exercise I have and how much I ate last. So I do best when I'm not coaxed or urged to eat more than I want.

After all, I'm supposed to gain only about four or five pounds over a whole year. That's only about six ounces a month!

You can help me a lot in my normal, healthy growing by giving me regular planned snacks, rather than all-day-long munchies. And by giving me water to drink for thirst rather than juice. And by not rewarding me with food, or giving me candy and sweets every day.

You can also help me a lot by encouraging me to run around and get sweaty. All that exercise makes me feel good and happy, which makes me even cuter.

If that's possible.

Day-care Grownups

Dear "Other Mother,"

You are my friend and teacher, and I want you to think I am the very best person in the whole world.

So as I grow, you are very important in teaching me how to exercise and eat in the way that keeps me healthy.

When you encourage me to run around every day and get all tired out playing, that helps a lot. Even if I'd rather play with dolls or trucks and draw pictures and read books, I need exercise to feel good and to grow the right amount.

When you put healthful, not-too-rich food out and let me decide how much of it to eat, that's a huge help. When I don't feel coaxed or urged, I can adjust my eating to my body's exercise and growing needs.

Because I could learn to eat from habit or because I am tired or bored or frustrated, I do best when you give me meals and snacks at regular times and don't let me nibble on munchies all day.

When you give me water instead of juice to drink between meals, I learn to drink when I'm thirsty, rather than because "it's sweet."

When you give me your smiles and happy words instead of food as rewards, I learn that food is "just food," and not the Ultimate Prize. When you don't use dessert as a reward, I learn that the rest of the meal is just as delicious as the sweet treat at the end—and I don't regard the dessert as the point of the whole meal.

You mean a whole lot to me, and I want to stay the apple of your eye. Thank you for helping me grow up healthy.

FIVE TO PUBERTY

Grandparents

Hey Dudes!

This is your favorite kid talking. What I want to say is, you are doing great helping me grow into my old baby fat.

*Here's what you **don't** do that helps me out a lot:*

You don't hover over me like an NYPD helicopter when I eat, or glare or sigh when I take a second helping. That makes it easier for me not to take a third; I don't know why.

You don't tell me that I weigh too much as if the thought never occurred to me. Boy, do I hate it when people do that.

You're never sarcastic. Like, "Gee, do you think three pies are enough?" or "Are you sure that'll last you until snacktime?" Yuck!

You don't make me jealous of other kids by going on and on about how slim and graceful they are.

*Here's what you **do** do:*

You make me feel great about what I'm good at. You find things to praise.

You compliment me when I look good. And when I don't, you don't say anything. You don't buy me clothes that just make me feel terrible.

When you have us over for dinner, you make food that isn't fattening but that everybody likes, so nobody gets mad at me.

You laugh at my jokes and you tell your friends how cute and smart I am. So I overhear you doing it.

You let other people know by how you act that they shouldn't tease me or nag me.

You make me feel loved and liked and proud of myself.

Snacks

For every age group, there are two kinds of snacks: those with significant nutritional value (protein, vitamins, iron, calcium) and those without.

This is important because snacks have different nutritional meaning for different children.

Children who aren't at risk for extra chubbiness can snack on foods that provide just calories without having those extra calories turn into extra fat; they either adjust their appetite and activity levels, or they burn those extra calories off as wasted energy.

But children who are at risk for extra chubbiness need a different approach to snacks. They need to have the snacks be counted as part of their daily total intake of calories and nutrition. That is, the snacks count as tiny meals, contributing to the daily requirement of vitamins, iron, and calcium. There's not a great deal of room for "extra" calories on a regular basis.

For each age group, I list the traditional snacks by whether they are extra-calorie snacks or nutritious snacks. The age grouping is important because of safety—no sunflower seeds for infants or toddlers, for instance—and sophistication of taste: It's a rare fifth-grader who will regard an Arrowroot cookie with gusto.

I have placed in the "extra calorie" list some foods that do have nutritional value—some protein, vitamins, calcium, iron—but that value is insignficant compared with the caloric richness and fat content. This category includes processed cheese, cold cuts, meat sticks, and whipped peanut butter whether it be smooth or crunchy.

And I have placed in the "nutritional" list, in the school-age section, a few foods that aren't very nutritious but that are low in calories, satisfying, and popular.

To make nutritious snacks more appealing to older toddlers and preschoolers, try making a puree of fresh fruit for a nice messy dip.

Diet drinks are not a good idea. It's not the chemical additives and artificial ingredients that are the main problem; they're not that toxic. Nor is it so much that they, like other carbonated beverages, impair calcium absorption in prepubertal girls, right at the age when they need extra calcium.

The problem with diet drinks is that they are sweet and fill up the stomach with gas. Chubby-prone children can become used to those two sensations from drinking many diet drinks. In fact, they can start to feel that sweet-satiated and filled-up are normal states, and that deviating from normal—that is, not sweet-satiated and not filled-up—is alarming. This can lead to all kinds of dietary indiscretions—another good reason not to give these to very young children.

OLDER INFANTS

Extra-calorie Snacks

Unfortified apple juice, pear juice, grape juice
Applesauce
Processed cheese slices
Cream cheese
Graham crackers
Saltine crackers

Nutritious Snacks

Iron- and vitamin C–fortified juice (as a snack, not as a thirst-quenching beverage)
Banana
Avocado

Cheerios
Softened (microwaved or simmered) pieces of apple, pear,
  peach, other nonchokable fruits
Cooked potato and sweet potato
Iron-fortified breads and muffins
Water-packed tuna

TODDLERS

Extra-calorie Snacks
All of the ones under extra-calorie Infant Snacks, plus:

> Cold cuts
> Chicken sticks
> Turkey sticks
> Hot dogs
> Raisins (chokable, too!)
> Sunflower seeds (also chokable)
> Nuts (also chokable)
> Cookies
> Little goldfish crackers
> Anything with more than a dab of mayonnaise or catsup
> (and if you're going to just dab, why do it at all?)

Nutritious Snacks
All the ones under Nutritious Infant Snacks, plus:

> Safe, fresh fruits (peel, de-seed, and halve grapes)
> Safe, fresh veggies (no celery, frozen peas, anything
> chokable)
> Hard-boiled eggs
> Pinto beans, kidney beans
> Cottage cheese
> Yogurt
> Lean meats and poultry
> Unprocessed Swiss cheese
> Bagels, muffins, and bread made with iron-enriched
> flour
> Dry cereal with or without milk: iron fortified and not
> sugar coated

PRESCHOOLERS

Extra-calorie Snacks

All those previously mentioned, plus:

  String cheese
  Hot dogs
  Sodas
  Potato chips, corn chips, corn nuts, tortilla chips

Nutritious Snacks

All those previously mentioned, plus:

  Organic unwhipped peanut butter spread thinly (still a
    choking possibility)

SCHOOL-AGE CHILDREN

From kindergarten on, snacks aren't just snacks; they're social occasions. When a kid is with friends or classmates or teammates, any parental restriction on snacks will backfire. You'll find yourself facing a resentful and deprived person. The following list is what to stock for snacks at home only.

Extra-calorie Snacks

All those mentioned previously, plus:

  Candy, cake, cookies, pies, sundaes
  Ice cream
  Nuts of all kinds
  Peanuts
  Sunflower seeds

Nutritious Snacks

  Pizza
  Popcorn
  Pretzels
  Pickles
  Celery

Fast Food

What point is there other than guilt in knowing the calories and fat grams in McWhopperburgers and so on? If fast food is a rare or occasional treat and seen as a bit of an occasion, it makes sense to throw nutritional awareness to the winds. Have the heart's desire, so that afterward there's no feeling of being cheated. You can make the next meal fat free and virtuous and sponsor extra exercise, too.

But there are times when you do want to have some guidance. For instance:

• When you are choosing food for a child too young to insist on a preference, you can figure out what is most healthful and what an appropriate portion is.
• When your child eats a fast-food meal practically every day, and you pay for it, you can decide whether you will fund only choices that are more nutritious and lower in fat.
• When your child really does like a range of the offered foods, and you can tactfully support one decision over another.

Most of the fast-food chains now offer lower-calorie, lower-fat, higher-fiber fare, and these are advertised on the menu along with their nutritional profiles. Many are in the 200- to 300-calorie range with fat content within the recommended "30 percent of total calories."

However, they don't label the old beloved standbys for nutrition. So I will. I haven't included the calories of the Happy Meals or Fun Meals or other children's specials. A Happy Meal is a once-in-a-while treat that usually comes with a toy or prize or game and as such shouldn't be agonized over. (Oh, all right; they're about 500 calories, 180 of them fat.)

MCWHOPPERBURGER SPECIALTIES

At most chains, the big specialty burgers with cheese all contain about 600 calories, with about half those calories as fat. Jack-in-the-Box wins with its bacon cheeseburger supreme at 724 calories, 405 of them fat.

Three slices of bacon adds about 100 calories, about 80 of them fat.

Ordinary cheeseburgers run about 300 calories, about half of them fat.

Ordinary hamburgers run about 230 calories, with about a third of them fat.

Egg biscuit sandwiches vary, from the Egg McMuffin or Biscuit with Egg at about 350 calories, 180 of them fat, to the ones with sausage, which run between 400 and over 500 calories, 270 of them fat.

CHICKEN

A two-piece meal with mashed potatoes, gravy, cole slaw, and roll runs to about 650 calories, about half of them fat.

A plain fried drumstick is about 120 calories, a breast 200 calories, and a thigh about 250 calories. "Extra crispy" adds 50 calories a piece.

Nuggets run about 320 calories, about 60 of them fat.

SHAKES

Shakes run about 350 calories, about 80 of them fat.

FRENCH FRIES

Regular orders of french fries run about 200 calories, about half of them fat.

TACOS

Regular tacos run about 200 calories, about half of them fat. Taco salads run about 370 calories, with about half of them fat.

SANDWICHES (on regular bread, not croissants)

Ham and cheese, roast beef, chicken, and fish sandwiches run about 450 calories, nearly half of them fat.

PANCAKES

Hotcakes with butter and syrup but without bacon run about 500 calories, only 90 of them fat. Three lean slices of bacon adds 100 calories, about 80 of them fat.

Bibliography

BOOKS FOR PARENTS

Jablow, Martha M. *A Parent's Guide to Eating Disorders and Obesity.* From The Children's Hospital of Philadelphia. New York: Dell, 1992.

The author of this superior book discusses healthful patterns of eating and exercise with special emphasis on teenagers and young adults. Obesity is considered to be in some youngsters a form of an eating disorder. The emphasis, because this is for an older age group, is on losing weight, not growing into excess chubbines.

Kleinman, M.D., Jellinek, M.D. with Julie Houston. *Let Them Eat Cake! The Case Against Controlling What Your Children Eat: The Pediatrician's Guide to Safe and Healthy Food and Growth.* New York: Villard Books, 1994.

The authors, a pediatric gastroenterologist and a child psychiatrist, urge two messages difficult to reconcile: Stock your pantry with all sorts of goodies, including candy and cookies and cake; but encourage fruit as snacks and a fat-limited diet. Their take on chubbiness for any given child is that first, the child probably isn't chubby; if he is, he won't be hurt by it; and if he is being hurt by it, parents need to get professional help.

Satter, Ellyn. *How to Get Your Kid to Eat. . . But Not Too Much.* Palo Alto, Calif.: Bull, 1987.

Satter, Ellyn. *Child of Mine: Feeding with Love and Good Sense.* Palo Alto, Calif.: Bull, 1991.

These are excellent books on the feeding relationship by a dietician/family therapist. When it comes to obesity, as the author says, she sees only children and adults who already are obese and who are struggling to lose weight. She doesn't see the succeful ones who grow into the extra fat. This leads her to emphasize family dysfunction rather than other influences. Both books focus more on finicky eaters than on chubbiness.

PROFESSIONAL LITERATURE

REVIEW ARTICLES

Bandini, Linda G., and Dietz, William H. "Myths About Childhood Obesity," Pediatric Annals, Vol. 21 No. 10, October 1992, p. 647–653.

Dietz, William. "Factors Associated with Childhood Obesity," Nutrition, Vol. 7 No. 4 July/August 1991, pp. 290–291.

Rosenbaum, Michael, and Leibel, Rudolph L. "Obesity in Childhood," Pediatrics in Review Vol. 11 No. 2, August 1989, pp. 43–57.

Schlicker, Sandra, et al. "The Weight and Fitness Status of United States Children," Special Article, Nutrition Reviews, Vol. 52 No. 1, January 1994, pp. 11–17.

RESEARCH STUDIES

Abraham, S., and Nordsieck, M. "Relationship of Excess Weight in Children and Adults," Public Health Report, 1960: 263–273.

Birch, Leann L., et al. "The Variability of Young Children's Energy Intake," New England Journal of Medicine, Vol. 324 No. 4, January 24, 1991, pp. 232–235.

Charney, E. "Childhood Antecedents of Adult Obesity," New England Journal of Medicine, Vol. 295 No. 1, July 1, 1976, pp. 6–9.

Committee on Sports Medicine and Fitness. "Fitness, Activity, and Sports Participation in the Preschool Child," Pediatrics, Vol. 90, 1992, pp. 1002–1004.

Davis, Kathie, and Christoffel, Katherine Kaufer. "Obesity in Preschool and School-age Children," Arch. Pediatr. Adolesc. Med., Vol. 148, December 1994, pp. 1257–1261.

Du Rant, R. H. "The Relationship Among Television Watching, Physical Activity, and Body Composition of Young Children," Pediatrics Vol. 94 No. 4, 1994, pp. 449–455.

Flodmark, Carl-Erik."Prevention of Progression to Severe Obesity in a Group of Obese Schoolchildren Treated with Family Therapy," Pediatrics, Vol. 91 No. 5, May 1993, pp. 880–884.

Fuchs, G. J. "Effect of Dietary Fat on Cardiovascular Risk Factors in Infancy," Pediatrics, Vol. 93 No. 5, May 1994, pp. 756–762.

Garn, S. M., Ph.D. and Clark, Diane C. "Trends in Fatness and the Origins of Obesity," Pediatrics, Vol. 57 No. 4, April 1976, pp. 443–456.

International Food Information Council/The American Dietetic Association. "How Are Kids Making Food Choices?" Washington: 1991.

Johnson, Susan L., Ph.D., and Birch, Leann L., Ph.D. "Parents' and Children's Adiposity and Eating Style," Pediatarics, Vol. 94 No. 5, November 1994, pp. 653–661.

Jopling, Joe, M.D. "Getting Families to 'Eat Right,'" Contemporary Pediatrics, May 1992, pp. 97–118.

Klesges, R. C. "Effects of Television on Metabolic Rate: Potential Implications for Childhood Obesity," Pediatrics, Vol. 91, February 1993, pp. 281–286.

Mallick, H. J. "Health Hazards of Obesity and Weight Control in Children: A Review of the Literature," Am. J. Public Health, 1983: 73: 78–87.

Robinson, Thomas, et al. "Does Television Viewing Increase Obesity and Reduce Physical Activity? Cross-Sectional and Longitudinal Analyses Among Adolescent Girls," Pediatrics, Vol. 91 No. 2, February 1993, pp. 273–280.

Rosenbaum, Michael, and Leibel, Rudolph. "Obesity in Childhood," Pediatrics in Review, Vol. 11 No. 2 August 1989, p. 53.

Sark, O., Atkins, E., Wolff, O. H., and Douglas, J.W.R. "Longitudinal Study of Obesity in the National Survey of Health and Development," Br. Med. J. 1981: 283: 13–17.

Shapiro, Leona, et al. "Obesity Prognosis: A Longitudinal Study of Children from the Age of 6 Months to 9 Years," AJPH, Vol. 74 No. 9, September 1984, pp. 968–972.

Shea, S. and Stein, A. D. "Variability and Self-Regulation of Energy Intake in Young Children in Their Everyday Environment," Pediatrics, Vol. 90 No. 4, October 1992, pp. 542–546.

Stunkard, A., and Mendelson, M. "Obesity and the Body Image, I: Characteristics of Disturbances in the Body Image of Some Obese Persons," Am. J. Psychiatry, 1967: 123: 1296–1300.

Sullivan, Susan A., Ph.D., and Birch, Leann, Ph.D. "Infant Dietary Experience and Acceptance of Solid Foods," Pediatrics, Vol. 93 No. 2, February 1994, pp. 271–277.

U.S. Department of Health and Human Services, "1985 President's Council on Physical Fitness and Sports Youth Fitness Survey." Washington: U.S. Government Printing Office, 1986.

Index